Ethics and
Belief

Ethics and Belief

Peter Baelz

A CROSSROAD BOOK
The Seabury Press
New York

1977
The Seabury Press
815 Second Avenue
New York, N.Y. 10017

Printed in the United States of America

Library of Congress Cataloging in Publication Data

Baelz, Peter.   Ethics and belief.
(Issues in religious studies)
"A Crossroad book."
Bibliography: p.   Includes index.
1. Religion and ethics.   I. Title.
BJ47.B33   1977   241   76-15425   ISBN 0-8164-1229-4

CONTENTS

General editors of this book
and others in
the *Issues in Religious Studies* series:
Peter Baelz and Jean Holm

1

MORALITY IN QUESTION

A moral problem is first and foremost a practical problem, although not all practical problems are moral problems. 'How do I get from Paddington to Waterloo by underground?' is a practical problem, but it does not appear to raise any obvious moral issues. A moral problem is concerned with right and wrong, with what ought or ought not to be done in these or those circumstances. 'How do I get from Paddington to Waterloo by underground without buying a ticket?' is also a practical problem. There are, no doubt, ways and means. Perhaps for some people it is never anything else than a practical problem. Someone, however, might say to me that it was wrong to travel by public transport without paying the correct fare, and that I ought not to do it. The practical problem has become a moral problem. A moral argument may begin. Or I may agree with him and admit that what I was trying to do was morally wrong and that I feel ashamed of myself.

Other examples of moral problems easily spring to mind, some of them private and personal, others public and political. For example, 'Ought I to sleep with my boyfriend when I don't really want to, but when he tells me that I am being silly and that I don't really love him if I refuse?' Or, 'Ought I to tell the police that my brother John is involved in a drug-smuggling racket?' Or, again, 'Ought I to campaign for spending a larger proportion of our national income on giving aid to underdeveloped countries when this will involve a heavier burden of taxation on everyone?'

Our moral judgements lead to decisions and actions for which we are morally responsible. Once we admit that we are confronted by a moral problem there is no way of side-stepping it. To shut our eyes and do nothing about it is itself a moral

1

decision for which we must accept responsibility. We cannot evade our moral responsibility simply by saying that it is none of our business. Of course, there are some matters which are in fact none of our business, and then it would be wrong for us to try to interfere. In these cases a decision to stand back and do nothing would be a morally responsible decision.

MORALS AND ETHICS

Moral problems, we have said, are practical problems. What about *ethical* problems?

Usage varies. The words 'moral' and 'ethical' sometimes have much the same meaning. It is useful, however, to try to preserve some kind of distinction between them, even if we are not always successful. So, for our purposes, ethics may conveniently be defined as the study of morality.

Ethics, then, is a reflective, or theoretical, business. It aims in the first instance at understanding rather than decision. It takes stock of the moral scene. It steps back from the immediately practical and attempts to discover some underlying pattern or order in the immense variety of moral decisions and practices both of individuals and of societies.

Ethics can be either *descriptive* or *normative*.

Descriptive ethics, as the phrase suggests, simply describes what is the case. It is a kind of natural history of morals. It tells us, for example, what moral rules and practices prevail in a particular society, or what moral principles are subscribed to by a particular individual. Descriptive ethics makes us familiar with the idea that there are numerous different moralities, such as Christian morality, or Buddhist morality, or middle-class morality, or Victorian morality. What is considered morally right in one society may be considered morally wrong in another society. What is considered the ideal of human excellence in one age may be considered far from ideal in another age.

In becoming alert to all these differences, however, we must be careful not to overlook more subtle and less obvious similarities. We are so conscious today of the wide variety of cultures, each with its own moral codes and customs, that we may fail to observe certain underlying harmonies between different cul-

2

tures. The question must be asked: Is there a larger measure of trans-cultural moral agreement than first meets the eye?

Different moral practices may express similar values. For example, in one society it may be considered the right thing to say exactly what one thinks of another person, while in another society it may be considered wrong to do so. On the surface it would seem that in the one society it is right to tell the truth, in the other society that it is right to tell a falsehood. What could be more different? On further investigation, however, it might turn out that both societies share a common respect and concern for the well-being and happiness of their members. Thus the difference may not be one of fundamental values so much as one concerning the best method and practice of expressing those values. The different rules have the same point.

Descriptive ethics tells us what patterns of morality actually exist. It does not attempt in any way to evaluate these patterns and to adjudicate between them. Normative ethics, on the other hand, does attempt some sort of adjudication. It makes proposals for what it considers to be the best ordering of morality. It suggests, for example, moral principles to be observed in sexual relationships, or in business affairs. It does not describe what is 'normal' in the sense of what is customary, or generally acceptable. It sets up a 'norm', or standard, with reference to which generally accepted principles and practices may be assessed. Thus a profession like the medical profession has its ethical committee to determine the proper standards of professional behaviour for its members.

Whoever engages in normative ethics is bound, sooner or later, to face a number of questions such as the following. Where does the proposed norm come from? For whom is the norm valid—for a particular group of people who for one reason or another are prepared to recognize the authority of this norm; or for all men everywhere simply because they are human beings sharing a common humanity, whatever their religious or political allegiance may be, whatever their race, colour or class; or only for the individual himself who sets up the norm? Are moral norms like tastes, or personal opinions, so that we expect, and even welcome, a variety of different moral standards and points of view, and do not feel alarmed or distressed by the fact that

3

my moral standards are not the same as yours, and your moral standards are not the same as the next person's? Or do we expect and look for agreement in moral norms, so that we can appeal to them over against our conflicting opinions, inclinations and desires, because they have an impartiality and reasonableness which give them an authority all of their own? Are my moral norms 'true for me', but not necessarily 'true' for anyone else? Or, if they are in any intelligible sense 'true' at all, have they a wider, perhaps a universal, claim to recognition?

These questions, and others like them, make up another kind of ethics, sometimes called *philosophical* ethics (or meta-ethics). In asking, for example, what kind of norm a moral norm might be, we were not describing some accepted moral norm, nor were we proposing a new moral norm of our own. We were doing something quite different. We were asking a prior question concerning the characteristics of moral norms in general. That is, we were asking about the linguistic and conceptual tools of the moralist's trade.

Philosophical ethics analyses the basic words and concepts of morality, such as right and wrong, duty, obligation, virtue, responsibility, etc., and traces their logical connections. These concepts have a logic, or pattern, of their own. To trace this pattern is not to make moral judgements about the rightness or wrongness of this or that act or practice, but to discover what are the rules which have to be observed if moral judgements are to form a rational and coherent part of moral argument. Arguments may be good or bad, convincing or unconvincing; but if they are to get off the ground at all, they must at least make sense. Thus understanding these basic moral concepts and their connections is something different from moral sensitivity and insight. It is like knowing the rules of cricket, whether one is any good at playing the game or not. If one wants to play the game at all, one must know the rules. It is the rules that make cricket the game it is. But knowing the rules will not by itself help one to score a hundred or get a hat-trick.

It is not universally agreed whether philosophical ethics is a descriptive or a normative study. If we took up again the analogy of playing cricket, we might be disposed to say that philosophical ethics must be a descriptive study. In cricket,

4

whatever the styles of batting and methods of bowling, the rules remain the same. Someone can describe them for us exactly as they are. In the same way it has been argued that, while moral judgements may differ from person to person and from society to society, the basic concepts and logical structure of moral argument remain the same. Thus philosophical ethics is said to be a morally neutral subject for study, leaving everything exactly as it finds it, simply describing the rules of the 'moral game', but not taking sides.

This argument that philosophical ethics is a descriptive study sounds convincing until one remembers that the rules of cricket do sometimes, even if only rarely, change. They are changed because an influential body of people has decided that a particular change will improve the game. So what we have to ask ourselves is whether there are any agreed rules in the 'moral game', or whether the rules themselves admit of more than one interpretation. If so, then the claim to be philosophically neutral may be something of a delusion. We may have to choose between competing descriptions of the way in which moral discourse ought to proceed, and choice introduces normative considerations.

What considerations will determine our choice? There are many. We may, for example, hold strongly to the view that some sorts of action, such as torture, are morally wrong whatever the consequences may be. If so, then we shall not be willing to accept a description of the rules of moral argument which affirms that the rightness or wrongness of an act is to be judged solely in terms of its consequences for good or evil. Thus our ethical theory will not be morally neutral. It will depend, at least in part, on some of the moral beliefs that we already firmly hold.

We have, therefore, to bear in mind the possibility that our philosophical ethics will be influenced by a wide range of moral and metaphysical beliefs, that is, beliefs about what it is to lead a truly human life and beliefs about the ultimate nature of the world in which men have to work out their destinies. In the last resort it may not be possible to isolate ethics from other studies such as politics or religion. What we believe to be the basic nature and structure of morality may depend, at least in part, on the total vision that we have of the world and of the kind of life, individual and social, which in the world as we see it is likely to fulfil man's deepest needs and potentialities.

It is precisely the connections which seem to hold between a man's opinions and his other beliefs which have given support to the view that morality is involved in an inevitable *relativism*. People's moral beliefs, it is said, depend on their upbringing, or on the social class to which they belong, or on the religion which they practise. If you believe that it is wrong to drop litter in the countryside, it is because you have been brought up to believe that it is wrong. Had you been brought up in a different family, it is more than likely that you would have seen nothing wrong in it at all. If you do not think that there is anything wrong with blood sports, it is because you belong to a social class in which blood sports are accepted as an exciting and harmless recreation. If you did not belong to that social class, you might think otherwise. If you are a Roman Catholic, you will probably see nothing morally objectionable in a regular weekly flutter on the football pools. If, however, you are a Methodist, it is more than likely that you will consider all forms of gambling morally objectionable.

Nothing that we have said so far is either surprising or disturbing. Of course people's moral beliefs are influenced by their upbringing, by the beliefs and attitudes of their parents, their teachers, their friends, and so on. But that is also true of many, if not most, of their other beliefs. Man is an imitative animal, and more often than not he picks up his beliefs and attitudes secondhand. Sometimes individuals come to reject what they have been taught. Even then this rejection is quite likely to arise out of a strong desire to imitate someone else, rather than out of a careful and dispassionate consideration of conflicting beliefs and a reasoned and deliberate choice of one and rejection of another.

However, the argument can be made more incisive. If one wishes to give an account only of the *causes* of people's moral beliefs, that is, how they came to acquire the beliefs that they do in fact hold, then it is often sufficient to point to the influence, open or hidden, of others. What, however, is the position if one asks after the *reasons* for a person's moral beliefs?

The person himself may not be able to give any convincing reason why he holds the beliefs that he does. He accepts them, he says, on good authority. No doubt the authority which he recognizes has its own perfectly valid reasons. When, however, we turn to the authorities, we discover that the so-called authorities differ among themselves. They have their reasons, but each authority appeals to a different set of reasons. What one authority thinks is eminently reasonable does not seem reasonable at all to another authority. How can this be? It is not necessarily the case that someone has made a mistake in his reasoning. The reasoning, so far as it goes, may be coherent and unexceptionable. But all reasoning has to start from somewhere. There have to be premises which are taken as self-evident and accepted without question. It is about these ultimate premises that the different authorities disagree. What is self-evident to one is far from self-evident to another.

It would appear that moral argument has only a limited chance of reaching an agreed conclusion. In the end, it seems, one simply has to appeal to different people's feelings, intuitions and insights. People may claim that their intuitions and insights give them access to moral truth, to what is actually the case. But people's moral intuitions conflict with one another. How, then, are we to decide which intuition is correct and which is incorrect? Where different people claim to 'see' things differently, and there is no agreed method of establishing which of them is in fact 'seeing' what is there to be 'seen', and which of them is only imagining what he claims to 'see', have we not good reason to think that the language of insight and intuition, when applied to morality, may be misleading? In the physical world we have, at least in principle, if not always in practice, methods of checking whether a person is actually seeing what he claims to be seeing. In the 'moral world', however, it is just these methods that seem to be lacking. Are we then mistaken in thinking and speaking of a moral 'world' at all? Does everyone live in his own 'moral dream-world'?

We shall return in the next chapter to the question of the validity and limitations of moral reasoning. Here, however, we note that we have brought to the surface what is in fact a fairly deep-seated suspicion, namely, that moral reasoning gets you nowhere, that there is little point in arguing about moral values, that in matters of morality one man's opinions are as good as another's, that every man is his own authority.

This suspicion is sometimes loosely expressed by saying that morality is 'subjective'. However, this expression is best avoided, as its meaning is too slippery to be of much use. In some contexts the distinction between 'subjective' and 'objective' may be reasonably precise. For example, if we say that the vase on the table is green and weighs a kilogram, we are speaking directly about the vase and describing it in a way in which others can quickly check whether what we are saying is or is not the case. Here there is no room for serious disagreement. We may properly be said to be speaking 'objectively'. If, however, we say that we like the vase and wish it were ours, we are no doubt referring to the vase on the table when we speak in this way, but first and foremost we are describing our own feelings and desires. We are speaking 'subjectively'.

Problems arise, however, when in talking about something other than ourselves and our own feelings we are thrown back on our own individual judgements. In many situations there are no public and impersonal ways of checking our individual judgements. Before the camera was invented, only the trained eye could be relied on to decide which horse was the winner in a neck-and-neck finish. The judges had to make their own judgements. And even the best and most experienced judges can sometimes disagree among themselves. Should we then call their judgements 'subjective'? Not if we keep to the usage suggested above, since none of the judges was speaking about himself and his own feelings. Certainly they were all using their own perceptions in order to make their judgements. They had nothing else to go on. But they were not speaking about their own perceptions; they were speaking about the horses that were running neck-and-neck.

If we still wish to use the word 'subjective' in order to stress the fact that there was no public and impersonal way of settling the dispute between the judges, and that the best that we could do would be to take the verdict of the majority, then we must remember that there are large areas of knowledge in which we regularly rely on 'subjective' judgements for determining what is true and what is false. The skill of judging has to be learned. Although we may not be able to appeal to any public and impersonal test, we recognize a world of difference between a trained 'subjective' judgement and an untrained 'subjective' judgement. If this were not so, we could not speak of a 'good' judge in this or that matter. It is, therefore, simply untrue to say that, where 'subjective' judgements are concerned, one man's opinion is as good as another's. Yet this is what is often implied when somebody else's opinion is dismissed as merely 'subjective'. Hence we do well to avoid the word when we are doing ethics. It begs far too many fundamental questions.

Our discussion of the use of the word 'subjective' has been something of a digression. Before we digressed, we were voicing the suspicion that in matters of morality one man's opinion is as good as another's, and this suspicion remains, whether we use the word 'subjective' or not.

MORALITY AND MORALITIES

It has often been remarked that when, in the nineteenth century, many thinkers abandoned their Christian dogmatic beliefs, they still retained Christian moral beliefs. They remained convinced that there was some single, ordered and universally valid set of duties and obligations which could be recognized by all men of good will and intelligence and which could therefore be called Morality. Twentieth-century anthropologists, however, have shown that the facts do not support this conviction. They have broken down the one, universal Morality into a number of different moralities. Twentieth-century individualists have taken the process still further. They have broken down the coherent and cohesive social moralities into an amalgam of countless individual moralities. There are now as many moralities as there are human beings. It is up to every individual to choose his own values, to determine his own moral way of life, and not to allow himself to be submerged in the anonymity and impersonality of a social group. His fundamental moral duty is to be himself. To be oneself, in the sense of choosing one's own way of life, is,

9

the jargon goes, to live 'authentically'. Simply to reflect the values of others is to abrogate one's true individuality and freedom, and so to live at second-hand, or 'inauthentically'.

Clearly we shall have to consider later what is valid and what is invalid in this plea for individual freedom and the consequent demand that each person should be allowed to decide for himself his own morality. It undoubtedly possesses a strong and widespread appeal, especially for those who feel that their lives are hemmed in by all sorts of human constraints, and who therefore want nothing more—or so it seems to them—than to be left in peace to do their own thing. For the moment let us accept this cry for individual freedom and authenticity as it stands, and then ask ourselves how morality appears from this point of view.

When we are old enough to reflect on what we do and why we do it, we realize that we have already picked up a number of beliefs about what it is morally right to do and what it is morally wrong to do. We know, or think we know, what we really enjoy doing, and most of us in our heart of hearts take it for granted that it is a good thing for a person to do what he enjoys doing. However, we have learned in the course of growing up that there are things which we enjoy doing that we ought not to do, and things which we ought to do that we do not enjoy doing. Hence morality—the morality which we have been taught—seems to consist of imposed restrictions on our natural inclinations.

Why, we ask ourselves, are these restrictions placed upon our freedom? The orthodox answer is that it is for the good of society, or, more paradoxically, for our own good. So we are placed in the position of inferiors, or of children, who do not know what is good for them, and who have to be directed by others who, it is alleged, know better than we do what is for our own real good. We have only opinions, and mistaken opinions too, while others have knowledge, and therefore the authority which is claimed to derive from knowledge.

But do those who claim to know really know? Of course there are experts in all sorts of fields of theory and practice, and often we have no hesitation in accepting the expert's instructions, even when we find it rather difficult to believe that his instructions are sound. But we do what he says, for he knows and we do not know. That is why we call him an expert.

What, however, are we to think of those who set themselves up as experts in morality? If individual freedom and choice lie at the heart of moral authenticity, can there even be such a creature as a moral expert? If there were, would that not mean that there was a fixed right and wrong which could be known to be right and wrong, and that the only freedom that the individual could claim would be the freedom to obey or to disobey? This would be a very poor sort of freedom compared with the freedom to choose one's own values and way of life.

Once again we are. approaching the fundamental question of the nature of moral values and of human freedom. Are moral values something to be *discovered*? Or are they something for each person to *invent* for himself? Is morality in some sense 'given', part of the furniture of the world in which man finds himself living? Or has man to 'create' his morality and to impose it on a world which is fundamentally indifferent to human values?

We shall postpone consideration of this difficult question until later. Let us for the present take as well founded the suspicion that those who claim to know what is true and what is false in the moral world do not really know any more than we know. Let us suppose that there is no moral truth to be known, no given moral world which would ground a moral truth in the way in which the physical world grounds a physical truth, so that our own opinions cannot make the physical truth other than it is. Why, if this is the case, do individuals and groups try to impose their own approvals and disapprovals on other individuals and groups?

THE INTEREST OF THE STRONGER

There is one possible answer to this question which puts morality in a very dubious light. It is that morality is the attempt of 'them' to impose their will upon 'us' in a manner which conceals from us, if we are not alert, the fact that this is what they are doing. Morality, that is, is a device for enabling one group of people to pursue its own interests at the expense of other groups. As early as the fifth century B.C. there appeared in the Greek-speaking world a number of professional educators, known as the Sophists, who taught that the laws and morals of a society were only

11

conventional, representing either the interests of those who were stronger, imposed upon those who were weaker, or the interests of those who were naturally weaker, but who had contracted together to protect themselves from those who were naturally stronger. Good and evil, right and wrong, were labels which different groups stuck on different actions and objectives. They had no universal and unchanging content. The whole system of morality was part and parcel of a process of indoctrination by which some men sought to get what they themselves wanted without being prevented by others who wanted something very different.

It was against this kind of teaching that the Greek philosopher Plato (*c.* 427–347 B.C.) argued in many of his dialogues. The example of his own revered teacher Socrates, who preferred to accept death rather than betray his deepest convictions concerning truth and goodness, was a living refutation of the sophists' teaching. In *The Republic*, which in F. M. Cornford's translation and commentary is still one of the most rewarding introductions to the study of ethics,[1] Plato sets out to analyse the whole nature of justice and righteousness in a society and in an individual, and in so doing is led to develop a fundamental theory of truth and goodness, knowledge and virtue, such as will make sense of the life and death of a man like Socrates, a truly good man.

None of us likes to be imposed upon. This is especially true in an age in which individuals and nations fight for their freedom, when those in positions of power and authority are called upon to produce their credentials, and when obedience is no longer the unquestionable virtue that once it used to be. It is, then, not surprising that, if indeed morality has no fixed content but reflects the interests only of those who promote it, its reputation is suspect. It professes to put forward considerations which should govern the actions of all men at all times. If, however, these considerations, despite their appearance, in fact reflect the values and interests only of the ruling class in its determination to hold on to its power, or only of parents in their desire to live their own lives again in the lives of their children, then the whole business is nothing but a sham. Beneath the façade of reason there is the

[1] F. M. Cornford, *The Republic of Plato.* O.U.P. 1941. See also J. E. Raven, *Plato's Thought in The Making.* C.U.P. 1965.

crude conflict of competing interests. Down with the mountebank Morality!

Why are we distressed at the suspicion that morality is a fraud? Is it simply because we have been duped for so long, that we have been trying to behave morally when we should have been joining in the free-for-all and fighting for our own interests? Or is it perhaps that we feel that there is something very wrong, something seriously inhuman, in the attempt of some to dominate and exploit others? If the former is the case, then we have woken up from a bad moral dream, have realized how foolish we have been to take moral considerations into account, and have determined in the future to look after ourselves and only ourselves. If, however, the latter is the case, then it looks as if we are rejecting 'morality' in the name of morality. False moral currency has been exposed by true moral currency. There is something 'wrong' and 'inhuman' about the naked pursuit of self-interest. Hence our suspicion of morality as a whole has been premature. We have been tempted to let false currency drive out the true.

In this chapter we have touched on a number of issues concerning both morality and ethics. Our purpose has been to provide some preliminary sketch of the territory which we shall be exploring. We have already raised questions concerning individual freedom and choice, authority and obedience, reasonableness and humanity. Our immediate task, however, must be to describe in greater detail what the idea of morality is all about. In other words, what is *a moral point of view*?

DISCUSSION QUESTIONS

Should we speak of morality (in the singular) or of moralities (in the plural)?

Should one expect ethical reflection on the nature of morality to have any practical value?

Is cannibalism moral in a cannibal country?

2

A MORAL POINT OF VIEW

Some say that morality has its ground and origin in the will of God, others in the order of society, others in an individual's free choice. Before we join in this argument we must try to get clear in our own minds what exactly we mean when we speak of a *moral* point of view.

PRESCRIPTIVITY

Moral problems, we have already suggested, are a kind of practical problem. Moral considerations, then, will be considerations which guide, or are expected to guide, our actions. Admittedly, there are few, if any, considerations which may not at some time or other bear upon our behaviour. For example, information about the differences between a grass-snake and an adder may, in the biology class, seem extremely remote and irrelevant. If, however, we come across a snake when we are out walking on the heath, this information may suddenly become extremely important for determining what we do. Moral considerations, on the other hand, are intrinsically, and not only incidentally, action-guiding. They have a direct and immediate bearing upon our actions. Hence the first thing to note about morality is that it is action-guiding. Moral considerations, it is sometimes said, are *prescriptive*. They tell us what to do and what not to do. They have something like the force of prescriptions, or commands.

Many different considerations have a direct bearing on what we do—considerations of what we feel like doing or want to do, considerations of what others, such as our parents or friends, suggest that we do or even tell us to do, considerations of what the law of the land requires us to do or what our religion appeals to us to do. From this wide variety we select and take into account only those considerations which seem relevant on any particular occasion. We allow now some, now others, to determine our actions. Moral considerations, however, seem to have, or claim to have, a certain *authority*. Some people argue that they have an overriding authority, that they take priority over all non-moral considerations. If I am convinced that something that I am thinking of doing is morally wrong, then I do not need to think of other reasons either for or against it. Indeed, other reasons for doing it become temptations. The fact that I want to do it, or the fact that others want me to do it, facts which in other circumstances would be good reasons for my doing it, are no longer good reasons at all. If I allow myself to be persuaded by them, I have given way when I ought to have resisted. I have failed to do my moral duty.

Moral considerations are often expressed in the language of 'ought'. We say that a man ought not to tell lies, that he ought not to be selfish, or that he ought to respect his parents. But not all 'oughts' are moral 'oughts'. We must be ready to distinguish between moral and non-moral 'oughts'.

Immanuel Kant (1724–1804) made the same basic point in the following way. He distinguished between hypothetical and categorical imperatives. Hypothetical imperatives are justified in terms of the ends, or purposes, which the actions are intended to achieve. Categorical imperatives need no justification in terms of human purposes. There is no 'if' about them.

Hypothetical imperatives include imperatives of skill and imperatives of prudence. 'You ought to keep your eye on the ball' is an imperative of skill. There is an underlying hypothesis that you want to play the game well. If you don't want to play well, then there is no need to keep your eye on the ball. Gaze at the sky, or at the spectators, if you desire. You will play the game badly; but if you don't mind about that, there is no more that needs to be said. The imperative loses its force. Similarly, 'you ought to go to the dentist to have your teeth looked at' is an imperative of prudence. The underlying hypothesis is that you want to keep your teeth in good condition. If you don't mind their decaying, with the result that you will suffer toothache, that is your concern. Again, the imperative loses its force.

15

Moral imperatives, however, are categorical. There are no 'ifs' about them. Your wanting, or not wanting, to do what the moral imperative prescribes is beside the point. 'You ought to tell the truth' is a categorical imperative. There are no 'ifs' and 'buts'. You ought—full stop. Moral imperatives claim for themselves an overriding authority.

At this point we must enter a certain *caveat*. Moral considerations may claim an overriding authority, and in normal circumstances this claim may be allowed to pass unchallenged. However, philosophers are not completely agreed on this point. It is not nonsensical to question the overriding authority of moral considerations. For example, an artist may admit that, morally speaking, he ought to spend more time and money in looking after his family. He may say, however, that his obligations as an artist override his moral obligations to his family. Whether we agree with his judgement or not, we at least understand what he is saying. He is not talking nonsense. So it appears that there are considerations which might conceivably be more authoritative than moral considerations. Or, again, a general in war-time might argue that the necessities of war are such that it would be wrong for him to be governed in his decisions by the moral considerations which he would count as supremely authoritative in times of peace.

Does it follow that moral considerations do not necessarily claim an overriding authority? It all depends on how you understand 'morality'. If morality is to be defined in part by its content—for example, by certain duties towards one's family or by certain standards of behaviour towards one's fellow men —then we might say that the artist and the general were acting contrary to their moral beliefs. If, however, morality is to be defined simply in terms of what a person, *all things taken into consideration*, believes that he, or anyone else in his position, *ought to do*, then both the artist and the general might be said to be acting according to their moral beliefs. The fact that a man is an artist, or a general, brings into play considerations which are not usually present and which make his moral duty different from that of a non-artist or of a peace-time politician.

So far we have suggested that moral considerations are (1) prescriptive, and (2) authoritative. We now introduce a third characteristic. This is the notion of *logical impartiality*, or, as it is often called, universalizability. This simply means that, if a moral consideration holds good for anyone, it holds for everyone in a similar situation. An illustration will help to make the point clear.

If I dislike or disapprove of smoking in a non-smoking compartment, I may express my disapproval with a frown. This may be little more than an immediate and unthinking physical reaction. Maybe, however, I say something, such as 'Disgusting'. I may even go so far as to ask the other person to put out his cigarette. If I do this, he may now find himself in two minds, whether to stop smoking or to carry on. So he asks me to give him a *reason* why he should stop. I could then give him one of a number of reasons. I might point out to him that we were both in a non-smoking compartment. Or I might say that I suffered from asthma, and that cigarette smoke was bad for asthmatic people. The reason for my asking him to stop smoking was, then, either that it was against the rules of the transport authority, or that it was wrong to cause unnecessary suffering to others. He might accept these reasons as valid, or he might not; but in offering him these reasons I was doing more than reacting in disapproval, I was pointing out to him the features in the situation on which I based my disapproval. I was inviting him, on consideration of these features, to share my disapproval. I was suggesting a reason which, if it was a good reason, would be a good reason for him, for me or for anyone else in a similar situation.

To claim that I have a good reason for adopting the attitude that I in fact adopt, or for issuing the command that I in fact issue, is to appeal beyond my immediate feelings and reactions to a more impersonal and less partial tribunal. A good reason for disapproving of smoking in a non-smoking compartment is a good reason, whether I am the person who is doing the smoking and you are the person who is doing the disapproving, or the other

17

way round. Reasons are impersonal, or inter-personal. They are logically impartial, or universalizable. A reason is in this sense like a law. A law holds good for anyone who comes within its orbit; it does not discriminate between John and James, or Mary and Susan.

Suppose, however, that when I was asked for a reason for requesting the other person to stop smoking, I had replied 'Because I say so'. I should simply have been repeating my previous request in a more threatening tone. I should not have been giving him a reason for what I was asking him to do.

Now let us return to directly moral considerations. Suppose that, when asked what reason I had for requesting the other person to stop smoking, I had said that he ought not to smoke because it was morally wrong. Was I, in using moral language in this way, giving him a reason, or was I simply repeating my command in different words?

It might seem that I was simply repeating my command in different words. To say that something is morally wrong invites the question 'Why is it morally wrong?' A reason still has to be given. Furthermore, parents are well known to answer, when pressed by their offspring with a series of whys, with the unanswerable 'Because I say so'. Nevertheless, it would be a mistake to think that I was adding nothing to my command by saying that it was morally wrong to do what I commanded should not be done. I was backing my command by an implicit appeal to moral considerations. I was affirming that there were good moral reasons for what I was saying, even if I could not myself give an altogether satisfactory account of these reasons and was compelled, in order to bring the conversation to an end, to appeal to authority, either my own or that of another.

It follows from all this that logical impartiality is a characteristic of a moral point of view. To adopt a moral point of view is to adopt a point of view for which, at least in principle, reasons can be given. Reasons, as such, are logically impartial, or universalizable. What is sauce for the goose is sauce for the gander.

Logical impartiality does not prescribe what the sauce shall be. If I think that it is morally right for me to pursue my own interests and to take no notice of the interests of others, I cannot be faulted for failing to observe the canon of logical impartiality so long as I am willing for everybody else to pursue his own interests and to take no notice of the interests of others, including mine. Logical impartiality prescribes that my moral principles shall be universally valid, but it does not prescribe what those principles shall be. It is not, therefore, to be equated with the particular moral principle of loving one's neighbour as oneself. Simply in terms of logical impartiality a principle of looking after oneself alone could count as a moral principle, so long as it included the right and duty of everyone else to be equally self-centred. Whether this would make practical, as contrasted with logical, good sense, human beings being what they are, is another matter. Such a principle, whole-heartedly and universally pursued, might lead to utter chaos and confusion.

So far we have suggested three characteristics which distinguish moral considerations from other kinds of considerations. Moral considerations are first, prescriptive, secondly, authoritative and thirdly, logically impartial. If I claim to be acting on a moral principle, rather than instinctively or merely selfishly, then I am claiming that my action is governed by a principle which prescribes what I am to do, has great, if not overriding, authority for me and, like any other rational principle, is logically impartial between one man and another.

All three of these characteristics refer to the structure of moral considerations, not to their content. We may say, therefore, in terms of a traditional philosophical distinction, that we have so far given a *formal* definition of morality rather than a *material* definition. We have described the shape but not the filling. There is nothing in what we have so far said to prevent a man from adopting whatever moral principles he chooses. An analysis like this has certain advantages. It does not rule out in advance, simply by definition, anyone's self-styled moral principles. The field is left wide open. If someone says that, all things considered, he is acting in the way in which he thinks it is morally right for him to act, then it must be granted that he is acting from a moral point of view, even if his action contradicts everything that we believe to be morally right and proper.

19

At this point, however, we may begin to feel a little uneasy. Have we been too open-minded? Should we not put some restrictions on the range of principles which we are prepared to recognize as moral principles? Must we not include some reference to content in our definition of morality? Has it not something essentially to do with other people's well-being, with the individual's relationship to society? If we think back to the example of the artist who in the pursuit of his artistic vocation neglects the interests of his wife and children, should we not say that, however fine his art, he was acting immorally? Should we not say that moral considerations were being subordinated to artistic considerations? We might dispute the point whether the artist was justified in acting as he did. We might even be prepared to concede that in certain circumstances morality must play second fiddle. But should we not hesitate to call the artist's decision to put his art before his family a *moral* principle?

Underlying our uneasiness is the feeling that morality has a specific content as well as a specific form, and that this is an inter-personal and social content. *Sociality*, we may feel, is as characteristic of moral considerations as is rationality. From this point of view egoism, the deliberate principle of seeking one's own happiness and only one's own happiness, is not a moral principle at all. It is the very opposite of morality; for morality, by definition, assumes a concern with other people's interests and needs. Acting selfishly is the contradictory opposite of acting morally, not one way of acting morally.

Selfishness could be defended as a moral principle on the grounds that everybody's interests are best served by each individual's pursuing his own interests. In fact this kind of argument has been used, not only in ethics, but also in economics. The good of society, it is alleged, is most likely to be achieved if everybody looks after his own good. Whatever the truth here may be, selfishness is not here acclaimed as an ultimate moral principle, but only as an instrumental principle which is morally justified in terms of its general consequences.

Ought we, then, to add a fourth characteristic to our list of those which distinguish moral considerations from other kinds of consideration? Ought we to say that moral considerations must be not only prescriptive, authoritative and logically impartial, but also *other-regarding*? Does a moral point of view take into account the interests of others, not only in so far as this is practically necessary for the pursuit of one's own interests, but also in their own right? In this case, if I adopt a moral point of view, I commit myself to a direct concern with other people's needs and interests. I adopt the viewpoint of an ideal observer, and my own interests thereby become those of only one among many. They do not have any special consideration simply because they are my interests and not those of someone other than myself. Some notion of justice and benevolence is thus built into the definition of morality. Morality has an essentially social function. Its impartiality is more than merely logical. It is an impartiality of attitude, intended to lead to an agreed resolution of conflicting interests through the recognition of principles of action accepted as binding upon all. Where there is no sense of justice and benevolence at all, no concern for the rights of the individual or the well-being of the community, moral considerations cannot begin to operate. If a man cares nothing for his fellow men, he cares nothing for morality, however 'moral' his behaviour may appear to be from the outside.

It seems to be the case that we have two overlapping but distinct usages of the word 'moral', the one individualistic and the other social. These two usages may reflect a tension in the developing understanding of morality. The original connection of the idea of morality with that of social custom[1] suggests that the social concept of morality is historically prior to the individualistic concept. In the course of history, however, individuals have from time to time stood out against the customs of society and have questioned the right of society to dictate to them what they ought and ought not to do. The rights of the individual have from time to time, especially in the Western Christian tradition, received predominant attention, so much so that at times the claim of the common good, deriving from the social aspect of morality, has tended to be overlooked.

This tension between the rights of the individual and the good

[1] 'Morality' is derived from the Latin *mores*, meaning 'customs'.

21

of society comes to be reflected in the ways in which the concept of morality is used. On the one hand we have the definition in purely formal terms, according to which moral principles are those principles of action which an individual, having taken everything into consideration, acknowledges as supremely authoritative. On the other hand we have the definition in social terms, in which moral principles are grounded in justice and the common good. According to the social definition conflicts of individual interest are to be resolved morally by taking 'a God's-eye point of view', that is, the point of view of 'an independent, unbiased, impartial, objective, dispassionate, disinterested observer'.[2] Thus morality has a god-like quality, whether a God's-eye point of view is actually occupied by God or not!

Common sense, I think, inclines towards a definition of morality in social terms. It assumes that the demands of morality may involve self-sacrifice. Duty and happiness do not necessarily coincide. In concerning himself with the needs and interests of others a man may have to forgo his own interests. The principles which it would be rational for him to adopt, if rationality is defined in terms of the consistent pursuit of what he himself ultimately wants, may conflict with the principles which he must adopt if he is to regard the common good as more important than his own good. Rationality and sociality do not always seem to point in the same direction.

In the following chapters we shall keep in mind both concepts of morality, the individual and the social, but shall incline to the common-sense view which, we have suggested, assumes that morality is essentially other-regarding. Thus a man who looks at things from a moral point of view is taken to be committed thereby to regard the interests of others, not only as they concern himself, but also as they concern them. He has in some sense to identify himself with others and to ask what he would want if he were in their shoes.

Before we proceed, however, let us at this point return to the question whether there is any value in arguing about moral beliefs, or whether each individual adopts his own moral beliefs

[2] See Kurt Baier, *The Moral Point of View*. Reprinted in G. Wallace and A. D. M. Walker, eds, *The Definition of Morality* (Methuen 1970), pp. 188–210.

and there is nothing further that can usefully be said.

THE ROLE OF ARGUMENT

If morality is other-regarding, then an individual's moral beliefs may be tested against the criterion provided by the social requirement that they take into account the needs and interests of others. The common good requires that there should be at least some harmony between conflicting interests, and this requirement creates the need for some kind of equity and justice. It also requires that there should be some consideration of the advancement of everyone's interests and the meeting of everyone's needs. Argument on these points is possible, and there is no reason why it should not be fruitful, even though it will not always be conclusive.

Furthermore, even if we subscribe to the individual concept of morality and allow that, when it comes to people's ultimate moral convictions, we may be faced with a number of conflicting beliefs which no argument can reconcile, this does not mean that all argument is useless in moral matters.

We have seen that a moral point of view, whether defined in individual or in social terms, takes a person beyond the mere expression of disapproval into an area in which he must support his disapproval with reasons. However and wherever his reasons may end, the fact that he is committed to giving reasons for his disapproval requires him to be consistent. It also requires him to be informed. These two requirements make it possible for argument to gain a purchase. Let us take the latter first.

Moral disagreement may in some cases depend on disagreement about the facts of the case and may be settled by reaching an agreement on what the facts are. Suppose, for example, that I say that smoking is morally wrong and you say that it isn't. I give as my reason for my moral belief the 'fact' that it causes cancer, and so distress to the smoker, his family and the community which has to care for him. You reply that there is no evidence that smoking does cause cancer; if there were, you would agree with me that it would be morally wrong. Our moral disagreement resolves itself into a factual disagreement.

Or suppose that I say that pre-marital sexual intercourse is

23

wrong and you say that it isn't. I give as my reason the 'fact' that it weakens the institution of lifelong marriage. You may reply that there is no evidence for this, and the disagreement becomes a factual disagreement. Alternatively, you may admit that this is probably true, but add that the institution of life-long marriage is a bad institution and ought not to be protected. Here the argument is no longer about the facts of the case but about the things that we believe to be valuable. If the argument is not to end at this point, I must give you my reasons for thinking that the institution of lifelong marriage is as valuable as I hold it to be. I may say that it is the best institution in which to bring up children; or that it offers the strongest base on which to build the most worthwhile personal relationship; or that it is part and parcel of my religion. Here, again, argument may proceed either on the basis of the facts or on the basis of moral principles and values. Where it is a disagreement about the facts, further argument is in principle always possible.

Or, to take a final example, I may say that capital punishment is morally wrong. I may argue that it fails to deter others from committing murder. This is a question of fact. Or I may argue that, even if it does have a deterrent effect, it is still morally wrong because the State has no right to take a criminal's life. This is no longer a question of fact. It is a question of moral principle, for which the facts about the deterrent effects of capital punishment are irrelevant.

Let us now turn to the other aspect of consistency. We should look for consistency both between our various moral principles and between our principles and our feelings of approval and disapproval.

For example, I may disapprove of bull-fighting. At the same time I may believe that there is nothing morally wrong with hunting. Can I be convicted of inconsistency? It depends. What is my reason for disapproving of bull-fighting? I may have a number of different reasons. I might, for example, believe that it absorbs passions and energies which ought to be given to political activity. If I did not believe that there was a similar objection to hunting, I should not be inconsistent in disapproving of bull-fighting and approving of hunting. If, however, my reason for disapproving of bull-fighting were that it causes unnecessary pain to animals, I should be guilty of an inconsistency if I saw nothing wrong with hunting. (The suggestion that foxes actually enjoy being hunted is too bizarre to be taken seriously!)

Again, I might claim to be a pacifist on principle. Should I be inconsistent if at the same time I believed as a matter of principle that murderers should be judicially sentenced and executed? If my reason for being a pacifist was that I held all human life to be sacred, so that in no circumstances had anyone the moral right to take the life of another, then I should be inconsistent if at the same time I approved of capital punishment. If, however, the reason for my pacifism was that war involved the killing of innocent people, especially women and children, then there would be no inconsistency in my not disapproving of capital punishment for convicted murderers—unless I took the view that there was always a risk that some innocent person might be wrongfully convicted and that this risk was sufficient moral justification for proscribing the death sentence.

None of us is consistent in his beliefs all of the time. Argument, therefore, has a use in exposing our inconsistencies. There may also be inconsistency between our principles and our feelings. I may, for example, hold as a principle the belief that the truth should always be told to patients who are suffering from terminal illness. Then one day I might be brought face to face with the actual consequences of acting upon this principle. I might be visiting a friend in hospital and discover that he had been told the truth about his physical condition and had gone completely to pieces. I might find myself instinctively blaming the doctor for telling him the truth. Yet the doctor had done something which, on principle, I believed to be morally right. What about consistency here?

I have a choice. I may either accept the force and validity of my immediate reaction and consequently have to modify my principle. Alternatively, I may stick to my principle, admit on reflection that the doctor had done the right thing and confess that my feelings, however natural, had to be discounted when taking everything into consideration.

We see now how experience and reflection both enter into a moral point of view. Our feelings, or intuitions, or reactions, are tested by being set within a larger context. Do they embody principles which, on reflection, I believe to be valid? Or are they only unreflecting responses which I have acquired willy-nilly and which call for thoughtful evaluation? Our principles are tested by being worked out in detail and their consequences tested against our feelings and intuitions. Thus there is a two-way process between the general and the particular, our principles and our immediate responses.

Perhaps it is worth remarking at this point how important a part the imagination may play in establishing a considered moral point of view. The novelist and playwright, by enlarging the bounds of our experience, enable us to test out, in imagination, our moral principles against all sorts of situations which we have not actually encountered. Should we still be prepared to subscribe to them in these or those particular circumstances? Or should we have to modify them, or even abandon them? The fact that these situations are imagined and not actual does not lessen their value for moral reflection, since our principles are intended to help us, not only in situations exactly like those which we have already encountered, but also in situations which differ from those which we have already encountered.

To sum up. In taking a moral point of view we are committed to the development of some kind of pattern of principles which shape and express our feelings of approval and disapproval. Some of these principles are perhaps ultimate; others are only intermediate. Even if our ultimate principles leave little or no room for argument, the same is not true of our intermediate principles. Here room for argument abounds, since they are based on other beliefs and principles to which appeal can be made.

If, as common sense seems to assume, morality is a social business, then argument is possible even about our high-level principles. We may argue whether they do justice to the 'other-regarding' aspect of morality and the requirements of the common good. We may be asked why we should take into account the common good, why we should be moral at all. Here, too, we are back with our fundamental attitudes. Can we give any reasons for their being what they are? Or must argument come to a final full-stop?

Before returning to the question 'Why be moral?' we shall take another look at the moral scene itself and examine two kinds of ethical theory which have been influential, the one concerned with acts and their consequences, the other concerned with agents and their motives.

DISCUSSION QUESTIONS

'All is fair in love and war.' Does this express a *moral* point of view?

'Our moral principles are only a rationalization of our instinctive approvals and disapprovals.' Do you agree?

Argue a case for and against corporal punishment. To what extent is factual information relevant to the argument?

3

ACTS AND AGENTS

A moral point of view, as we have defined it, is one that takes into direct account not only an individual's own interests, but also the interests of others.

Who these 'others' are is open to debate. A moral point of view is not always a universal point of view, from which all human beings, whatever their race, colour or intelligence, can be seen to merit equal consideration. It may be a more limited point of view, in the sense that it takes into account only members of the family, or members of the tribe, or members of the nation. One of the substantial moral questions which individuals have to answer is 'Who is my neighbour?' How far do the boundaries of the moral community extend?

In human history there has been a movement, partly moral, partly religious, to extend the moral community to include all human beings. It is a man's humanity, which he shares with all other human beings, which is acclaimed as the basis of membership in the moral community, not his being an Aryan, or a Jew, or an Arab, nor his being a Christian, or a Muslim, or a Hindu.

Even the concept of shared humanity raises questions. Ought we to acknowledge intelligent beings from another planet as members of the same moral community to which we, as human beings, belong? Have we any moral duties towards animals, not because they are intelligent, but because they have basic feelings of pleasure and pain not altogether unlike ours? Furthermore, the concept of humanity is blurred at the edges. Is an unborn foetus to be counted as a human being? And what of someone who, either from accident or from senile decay, is, to all outward appearances, no more than a 'vegetable'? It is no academic matter whether these are to be counted as members of the moral community or not. It can be a matter of life or death for them.

Leaving on one side questions about the extent of the moral community, we return to the consideration that a moral point of view is an impartial and disinterested point of view, to be distinguished from and contrasted with an individual's own partial and interested point of view. The question 'What ought I to do here and now?' is different from the question 'What do I want to do here and now?' Duty and interest often conflict. I may want to go to watch the football match, but I know that I ought to go and visit my aged and lonely aunt. Moral reflection introduces different considerations from those I take into account when I am concerned only with pleasing myself.

DUTIES AND RIGHTS

Moral considerations are expressed in a variety of ways. Sometimes we speak of our duties and obligations. We have at the back of our minds a list of such duties, those, for example, which we owe to our husbands, wives, parents, children, or to our friends and colleagues; or to our country; or to the Church; or, perhaps, supremely to God. We *owe* God our worship and obedience, we may say, if we have been brought up in a certain religious tradition. These duties stem from an ordered system of relationships. Consequently, the phrase has been used, 'My station and its duties'.

Other duties we recognize are more general. For example, we may say that we have a duty to keep promises, to act honestly, to obey the law and to help our neighbours. This list of duties can be extended to include more far-reaching and far-ranging behaviour. For example, we may acknowledge a moral duty to spend time and money on helping those whose needs are greater than our own. This might be called a duty of beneficence, or charity—a duty of giving help wherever help is needed and we ourselves are in a position to offer that help. Or, again, we may believe that we have a moral duty to develop our own talents and potentialities rather than let them lie around unused.

In moral discussion we speak not only of duties and obligations, but also of rights. Sometimes we refer to basic human

29

rights, and we urge men and nations to respect these fundamental rights and to acknowledge them in their laws. The most basic right of all, it would seem, is the right to life. If this right is overridden, the possibility of exercising other rights is removed. Because the right to life is so fundamental, we sometimes speak, in religious terminology, of the sacredness of human life. Other rights that are claimed to be basic include the right to freedom and the right to equality before the law. Thus 'freedom' and 'equality' became a kind of moral emblem, even when their meaning is not clearly spelled out.

'Rights' seem to multiply in a remarkable way. It is claimed that everyone has a right to work. If there is a fundamental right to live, there is also, it is sometimes said, an equally fundamental right to die. A woman has the right to decide what shall and shall not be done with her own body; and this is sometimes taken to imply that she has a right to an abortion if such is her wish.

So the list of rights seems to grow. But where do these rights come from? If they were only *legal* rights, we could answer the question simply: they originate from and are upheld by the law. But these rights which we have been talking about are claimed to be *human* rights, to exist prior to any legislation and to be taken into account when laws are made. Is there a more-than-human law, a divine law, in which these human rights are grounded? This would certainly be the answer of those who believe in God and also believe that he is the supreme law-giver. What, however, of those who do not believe in such a God and yet still wish to use the language of fundamental human rights?

Some argue that these basic rights are 'self-evident'. Anyone who stops to think can 'see' that these rights exist. They are as clear and compelling as the axioms of Euclidic geometry. (Does such an appeal to intuition and self-evidence lose some of its force when it is remembered that Euclidic geometry is not the only geometry, and that there are alternative geometries, with alternative axioms, which can be more useful for certain purposes?) Others claim these rights on the basis that they themselves, as individuals, feel passionately about them, and expect others to feel in the same way. Others, again, claim that these rights can be derived from a consideration of what it means to be a human being. Human beings differ from each other in all sorts of ways; but there is a basic set of characteristics which are of the essence of humanity and constitute an order of life any deviation from which would be less than human. This basic moral order gives rise to certain rights and duties. Men *can* ignore them; but if they do, they are morally bad men. Sometimes we may call them thoroughly *inhuman*.

CONSEQUENCES

It is not surprising, what with all this variety of rights and duties, some of which seem clear and indisputable to one group but not to another, and many of which seem on occasion to conflict with one another, that there has been a strong desire to cut through the muddle and mystification and to reduce the confusion to some sort of rational order. Is there not a simple and straightforward way of settling moral disputes, at least in principle?

Perhaps the simplest and neatest ethical theory is that of Utilitarianism, associated especially with the names of Jeremy Bentham (1748–1832) and John Stuart Mill (1806–73), but, in one form or another, still commanding considerable support.

What all men want is pleasure, or happiness. That is the common thread running through all human aims and objectives. The value of men's actions, therefore, is to be assessed in terms of the happiness that they produce. Just as the individual, when he has only himself to think about, makes up his mind what to do in terms of what will give him the greatest pleasure, or happiness, so the member of society, concerned with the interests of others as well as with his own, must make up his mind what to do in terms of what will produce the greatest happiness. My single and overriding concern in any conflict of interests will be so to act as to ensure that the greatest number of people enjoy the greatest amount of happiness. Thus, according to utilitarian theory, actions are to be judged right or wrong solely in terms of their consequences; and their consequences are to be judged good or bad solely in terms of the pleasure, or happiness, that they involve. All talk of natural rights was dismissed by Bentham as so much muddle; he called it 'nonsense on stilts'.

31

Utilitarianism is an attractive theory for a number of reasons. It is simple, intelligible and economic. It imposes an order and unity where previously there was plurality and disorder. It prides itself on sticking to the facts and keeping clear of fanciful notions and idealistic chatter. It appeals to the single motive of benevolence, the desire that people should be happy. In its negative aspect of refraining from causing unhappiness it finds implicit support in the question commonly voiced when something is declared to be morally wrong: 'Why, what's the harm?' For if no harm is caused by a particular action, there is nothing, according to utilitarian theory, which can make that action wrong. Furthermore, the application of the principle of utility to public affairs has provided a reforming weapon whereby entrenched positions of privilege have been destroyed and the well-being of the whole community has been made the primary objective of economic and political action.

On the other hand, utilitarianism has had to face a number of serious objections. For example, it has been argued that we cannot possibly know all the effects of our actions, and that therefore we can never know whether what we decide to do is morally right or wrong. Again, it has been objected that it is impossible to reduce the 'goods' which men seek to a single thing called 'pleasure', or 'happiness'; that we cannot reduce happiness to measurable and comparable quantities; and that in any case there are qualitative differences between different kinds of satisfaction. It was John Stuart Mill himself who acknowledged that it would be better to be Socrates dissatisfied than to be a pig satisfied.

These, and other, objections to utilitarianism are not necessarily conclusive, but in answering them the utilitarian is inclined to make such modifications in the theory that its original simplicity—which was one of its most attractive features— threatens to vanish.

For our present purposes we wish to point to two areas in particular in which utilitarianism has come under fire. The first concerns the matter of justice, the second the moral significance of the agent, that is, the person who is performing the action.

It is debatable whether principles of justice are compatible with the principle of utility. It may be argued that in the long run it is for the greatest happiness of the greatest number that every member of the community should be granted certain basic rights which considerations of public interest should not be allowed to override. In the short run, however, public interest can all too easily be allowed to ignore what is just.

What, for example, are we to say about Caiaphas' celebrated remark when, according to the Fourth Gospel, the chief priests and Pharisees were debating what to do about Jesus: 'It is expedient for you that one man should die for the people, and that the whole nation perish not'? Do considerations of public interest justify judicial murder? Or what are we to say about the decision of the British Government at the end of the Second World War to hand over to their Russian allies the nationals who had been fighting on the side of the Germans, even though they were as certain as they could be that by so doing they were sending them to their deaths?

Considerations of justice and of public interest may conflict. In these circumstances utilitarian considerations may seem to some to cloud rather than to clarify the real nature of the moral dilemma. In arguing that the promotion of general happiness, morally important as it undoubtedly is, must be contained within the limits of 'veracity and justice', Joseph Butler (1692–1752) did not hesitate to point out his brief *Dissertation on the Nature of Virtue* the numerous crimes which men might justify in the name of benevolence: 'It is certain, that some of the most shocking instances of injustice, adultery, murder, perjury, and even of persecution, may, in many supposable cases, not have the appearance of being likely to produce an overbalance of misery in the present state; perhaps sometimes may have the contrary appearance.'[1] For Butler 'the happiness of the world' was the proper concern of God, not of man.

If justice raises problems for utilitarianism, so too does the moral significance of the agent.

If morality is primarily about means and ends, then the moral significance of the agent is reduced to that of being the cause of certain consequences. His value is to be assessed in terms of the happiness that he produces. Human action is to be praised or

[1] J. H. Bernard, ed., *The Works of Bishop Butler*, vol. II (Macmillan 1900), § 10, p. 294.

blamed in so far as it promotes or hinders human happiness. Results are what count.

Now this emphasis on results, or consequences, however attractive it may be to the practical and public-spirited person, reflects only one aspect of morality. It shows no concern with the inner wrestling and integrity of the individual. It is wholly concerned with what goes on 'outside' the individual's heart and mind, with what is done rather than with the motive for what is done. The agent is to be valued according to his action; but his 'action' is only a cause of a rather complex kind. Morality is a kind of psychological machinery for getting a particular job done. It has a value only in so far as it serves a purpose. If there were any other machinery which could do the job more efficiently, then this should be substituted for morality. If, for example, the infiltration of a certain chemical into the public water supplies would so modify people's behaviour that they would behave less aggressively towards each other, then no one in his right mind should have any moral scruples about using this chemical. The resulting increase in human happiness would amply justify this interference with the 'rights' of individuals to decide their own actions for themselves. What is the value of individual 'freedom' if action by the State increases everyone's 'happiness'?

MOTIVES

There has, however, been an important ethical tradition which has located the core of morality, not in acts as such, considered simply as links in a chain of cause and effect, but in human action interpreted as expressing the agent's intentions and values. Morality is the expression of an inward form of life. Motives count for more, morally speaking, than achievement. Producing the goods, however desirable, is not the heart and soul of morality. Benevolence is undoubtedly a virtue; but is it the whole of virtue? Is morality only partly concerned with producing happiness? Or is it not specifically concerned with happiness at all? What are we to say of the person who does the right thing, from the point of view of its consequences, but does it for the wrong reason, or from the wrong motive?

This very different approach to morality has been strikingly

34

expressed in an essay by J. L. Stocks, entitled *The Limits of Purpose* :

> The utilitarian, who is the practical man turned philosopher ... means by action only a particular type of result, a result which is conditioned by conscious human activity. He cannot get away from results, for results carry the only independent value which he recognizes. Morality, however, like art, cares nothing for results. To morality it does not matter what the results may be, so long as they are practically acceptable. The future result must be transformed into the present intention before it will enter into the notion of action judged good or bad ... Justice is not altered though the heavens fall.[2]

This approach to morality stands in the tradition of what may be called an ethic of motive, as contrasted with an ethic of consequences. Morally speaking, an action must be judged from the agent's point of view, in terms of intention and motive, not from the manipulator's point of view, in terms of results and consequences.

Men have various purposes in life. They desire certain 'goods'. Purposive activity aims at making things in some way better. What counts as good will vary as men's desires vary. My good will probably not be the same as your good. All our goods could be reduced to a single and harmonious good only if the moral community to which we belonged were itself a single person rather than a community of different persons. It is a mistake, then, according to an ethic of motive, to think that it is the function of morality to harmonize conflicting interests by inventing another overriding interest. On the contrary, morality is concerned with means rather than ends, with the way in which men go about achieving their purposes. Some of these ways may be wrong, however admirable the purposes. Morality is concerned with a pattern of life rather than a goal.

This ethical tradition finds expression in a number of different ways. Sometimes it is said that 'right' and 'wrong' are the fundamental moral concepts, and that they cannot be analysed, as by

[2] J. L. Stocks, *Morality and Purpose*, ed. D. Z. Phillips (Routledge and Kegan Paul 1969), p. 30.

35

an ethic of consequences, in terms of 'good' and 'bad'. An action may produce a highly desirable and therefore good result, but it may nevertheless be morally wrong. It is no doubt highly desirable that the poor should be fed; it can be questioned, however, whether it is morally right to rob the rich in order to feed them.

Sometimes it is said that, although the moral rightness of an action cannot be analysed into anything more simple than itself, it can be described. It is like a claim. It exercises an authority over us, even if we do not always obey it. It is part and parcel of our ordinary human experience. Anyone who says that he does not recognize such a moral claim, and does not understand what 'right' and 'wrong' mean, is either a knave or a madman. It is a matter of direct 'seeing', of intuition. It is a form of intellectual awareness, of immediate knowledge. Everyone in his right mind knows what is meant by saying that cheating at cards, showing cruelty to children, punishing the innocent, are morally wrong, and at the same time recognizes the truth of what is meant.

Perhaps the most celebrated attempt to develop an ethic of motive, and at the same time to say more about the basic notion of moral rightness than simply that it is basic and that it can be recognized as such, was that of Immanuel Kant.

We have already had occasion to draw attention to Kant's distinction between hypothetical and categorical imperatives. For Kant the categorical imperative was not an ultimate and mysterious claim that came, as it were, out of the blue. It was grounded in man's own nature as a *rational being*. It was independent of human desires, which changed with changing circumstances. It was a criterion of action which rationality demanded, whatever a man might desire. It was a criterion which was valid for all rational beings.

Kant expressed this imperative in three different but complementary ways: 1. Act only on that maxim through which you can at the same time will that it should become a universal law; 2. Act in such a way that you always treat humanity, whether in your own person or in the person of any other, never simply as a means, but always at the same time as an end; 3. So act as if you were through your maxims a law-making member of a kingdom of ends. Thus in morality man is bound to impose a rational pattern on all his actions. They must reflect a principle of action which can be universalized. Furthermore they must treat all men as ends in themselves and not merely as levers in a system of desires and satisfactions. The first formula stresses the moral characteristic of logical impartiality and universalizability; the second and third formulae develop this in the direction of sociality.

If a morally right action is one that accords with the categorical imperative, the morally good person is one who does what is morally right *because* it is morally right, and not because he is otherwise inclined to this action or because he hopes to achieve something by it. The morally good person acts out of a sense of duty. Pity, compassion, love may be commendable human virtues; but respect for the moral law is the single and supreme moral virtue.

When Kant speaks of the moral law, it cannot be emphasized too often that this is no law imposed by an external law-giver, whether a parent, a ruler, or even God himself. It is a law which is the law of man's own being. Morality arises from the fact that man as a rational being imposes this law upon himself. His rational humanity is autonomous (that is, self-legislating) rather than heteronomous (that is, legislated by some other).

For Kant the essence of the moral conflict is not the struggle between egoism and altruism, the desire to further one's own happiness and the desire to further the happiness of others. Rather is it the demand that all our desires should be submitted to the approval of our rational judgement. There is no further arbiter to be consulted. The moral law is 'within'. It is the expression of the true ordering of ourselves. To act immorally is to act out of order. A kingdom divided against itself cannot stand.

Some critics of Kant have complained that his ethical theory is too formal and abstract, and that, in setting rationality over against desire, he has failed to do justice to the rich complexities of moral experience. Some feelings, they say, such as compassion, are an intrinsic part of moral goodness. Be that as it may, what is important for us to note here is his determination to ground morality in man's own being. What man ought to be is determined by what man is.

This method of approach to morality, namely, the attempt to discover what man ought to do and what he ought to be by reflecting on what he is, has a long and respectable history in ethical thought. However, there are many who believe that this approach is fundamentally wrong. They argue that it is logically impossible to derive an 'ought' from an 'is'. State any number of facts that you like about what is the case; nothing follows from this about what ought to be the case. Consequently any ethical theory which sets out to derive moral conclusions from facts about human nature is bound to fail from the start.

The strength of this objection is difficult to assess. Some consider it conclusive; others consider it only a verbal quibble. It is too complex a question to consider now. Perhaps we may be allowed to assume that some notion of what is good for man, and so what man ought to do and to be, can be gained from a consideration of human nature and human relationships. For example, it might be argued that men have certain basic needs, that the satisfaction of these needs is good for them, that there is something amiss if these needs are not satisfied, and that therefore they ought to be satisfied. Even if this argument is not logically watertight, at least we may think it reasonable to know as much about man as we possibly can, his needs and potentialities, if we want to find good reasons for saying that he ought to do this rather than that, or that he would be a better man if he had these characteristics rather than those.

Sometimes it is argued that, just as we can say what a good knife is when we know what a knife is for, so too we can say what a good man is when we know what a man is for. Again, just as we can see that there is a right way and a wrong way to use a knife, so we can see that there are right ways and wrong ways for a man 'to use himself'. Over against this it may be objected that we know what a knife is for; but does it make sense to speak of what a human being is for? If not, then there is nothing comparable to determine how a human being should behave and how he should not behave.

Let us return to human nature. Kant thought that man was

38

essentially a rational agent. Others have depicted him as essentially a pleasure-seeking animal. Yet others have discovered in human nature something too complex to be reduced to a single principle. For this last group morality consists in a proper ordering of human nature. Plato, for example, spoke of the three 'parts' of the soul, and depicted 'justice' as the proper ordering and integration of these three 'parts'.

Butler is another who demands that we do justice to the complexities of human nature—to the particular desires and inclinations which form the raw material for our actions, to the general principles of self-interest and of benevolence, and to the conscience which has the last word in ascribing to desires and principles their proper weight and function. In D. M. MacKinnon's words: 'Butler is the enemy of the single formula, whether it be the identification of virtue with benevolence, or with the proper balancing of benevolence and prudence, or with justice, or with pity, or with piety; it is none of these things; it is living in accordance with our actual nature.'[3]

If morality, as moralists of this tradition hold, is grounded in our actual nature, then we must gain every insight that we can into that nature. We shall need to take note of what the biologist, the psychologist and the sociologist can tell us from their studies in the human sciences. But we shall also need to take note of what the historian, the novelist and the poet can reveal to us; for they too have their important insights.

For Butler, living in accordance with our actual nature involved paying special attention to the conscience. But what is the conscience? Has it in fact the importance and authority which Butler, for example, ascribes to it?

DISCUSSION QUESTIONS

Discuss the use of 'pleasure' in the following sentences: 1. He lives only for pleasure; 2. John and Mary Smith request the pleasure of your company at the marriage of their daughter; 3. I will wait upon his pleasure.

Does it make any difference what the motives of a public bene-

[3] D. M. MacKinnon, *A Study in Ethical Theory* (Adam and Charles Black 1957), p. 181.

factor are so long as his benefaction is substantial?

> This is the last and greatest treason
> To do the right deed for the wrong reason.
> (from T. S. Eliot's *Murder in the Cathedral*)

Do you agree?

4

A MATTER OF CONSCIENCE

Some people get impatient with long-winded moral arguments, which seem to them to complicate what is essentially simple and to obscure what is eminently clear. They begin to suspect that all these arguments are sophisticated attempts to drown the clear voice of conscience. Surely, they say, there is no problem about knowing what ought to be done in a particular case. A person's conscience tells him what he ought to do and what he ought not to do. The only problem they see is that of actually doing what one's conscience indicates. It is a problem of obedience, not of knowledge. The voice of conscience is not the only voice that can be heard. There are other voices tempting a person to act against his conscience. And these other voices are expert at producing long and complicated arguments intended to show that there are 'good reasons' for not doing what he knows he ought to do.

What is the conscience? We speak of conscience in a variety of contexts. We say, for example, that some things are a 'matter of conscience', meaning thereby that they cannot be settled by ordinary prudential considerations of what is expedient, or by a majority verdict which is binding on everyone, but that they raise fundamental moral issues and that each individual must be allowed to think and act as seems morally right to him. Again, 'conscientious objectors' in war-time are those who profess that they have a fundamental religious or moral objection to taking part either in any war or in this war in particular. In some countries they are imprisoned, or even executed, for their refusal to fight; in other countries their conscientious objection is respected.

Some people seem to pride themselves on 'having a conscience', others on not having a conscience. We speak of 'pangs of conscience' and of a 'guilty conscience'. It often seems as if a man's

41

conscience is more interested in keeping him from doing wrong than in encouraging him to do what is right: a good conscience comes to mean the absence of a bad conscience! Sometimes we show surprise when someone betrays no signs of suffering from a guilty conscience. We may exclaim: 'Don't you have a conscience?'

'Conscience', then, seems to refer to something within us. Yet it is not altogether a part of us. It can stand over against us, so that it seems almost to have a separate existence of its own. It can condemn us. It can command us. It is not, then, surprising that it has sometimes been described as the 'voice of God'. Milton's God expresses this view as follows: 'And I will place within them as a guide My umpire Conscience'.[1] At other times it can seem anything but the voice of God. It is like a sickness or disease, so that we suffer from uncontrollable feelings of guilt, even when we do not think that we have anything special to feel guilty about.

BUTLER'S IDEA OF THE CONSCIENCE

Butler, as we saw in the last chapter, ascribed to the conscience the final say in moral decisions. He argued that a proper regard for human nature required that consideration be given to the natural instincts and affections which form the raw material of our humanity. These, however, need to be given shape and direction. They have to be ordered according to some rational principle. He mentions two principles, those of prudence, or self-interest, and of benevolence, or interest in the happiness of others. These principles, he asserts, are not contradictory; but, human nature being what it is, although more often than not they point in the same direction, at other times they may point in different directions. Thus human inclinations, even when ordered according to rational principles, sometimes conflict. In cases of conflict we need some way of settling the conflict. At this point the conscience comes into play. Here is the final moral authority. Whenever there is a conflict between prudence and benevolence, or between justice and pity, or between the claims of family and the claims of the wider community, the conscience must be the

[1] *Paradise Lost*, III, 194–5.

42

final arbiter. It knows, in any particular situation, what is the morally right thing to do.

> Thus that principle, by which we survey, and either approve or disapprove our own heart, temper, and actions, is not only to be considered as what is in its turn to have some influence; which may be said of every passion, of the lowest appetites: but likewise as being superior; as from its very nature manifestly claiming superiority over all others: insomuch that you cannot form a notion of this faculty, conscience, without taking in judgment, direction, superintendency. This is a constituent part of the idea, that is, of the faculty itself: and to preside and govern, from the very economy and constitution of man, belongs to it. Had it strength, as it has right; had it power, as it has manifest authority, it would absolutely govern the world.[2]

Conscience, for Butler, is king, but a constitutional king. It maintains the moral order of human nature, but it allows proper expression to all aspects of human nature. It takes into account even the 'lowest' of human desires. These, too, have their place in the order of our true humanity. They are not to be suppressed and destroyed in the name of some 'higher' rationality or spirituality. Rather, they are to be ordered aright. At the same time they must acknowledge the right of conscience to give them their due place; they do not possess this right themselves, however powerful they may be.

Butler is more concerned to describe the place of conscience in moral experience than to explain its source and ground. In modern jargon we might say that he was giving us a phenomenology of conscience rather than a metaphysic of conscience. At the same time, however, he not only describes the way in which conscience claims authority, he also acknowledges the propriety of the claim, whatever 'conscience' in the last analysis of things may turn out to be. In his *Dissertation on the Nature of Virtue* he writes:

[2] From Sermon 2, *'Upon Human Nature'*. See J. H. Bernard, ed., *The Works of Bishop Butler*, vol. I (Macmillan 1900), p. 48.

That we have this moral approving and disapproving faculty, is certain from our experiencing it in ourselves, and recognising it in each other ... It is manifest great part of common language, and of common behaviour over the world, is formed upon supposition of such a moral faculty; whether called conscience, moral reason, moral sense, or Divine reason; whether considered as a sentiment of the understanding, or as a perception of the heart; or, which seems the truth, as including both.[3]

For Butler human beings without the faculty of conscience would hardly be human beings at all.

It is not altogether easy to see exactly what Butler is after. He always prefers to admit the complexities of human experience rather than to achieve a systematic consistency at the cost of distortion of the facts. However, we can, I think, point out two fundamental features of his thought.

First, when he speaks of the conscience, he is not thinking of some alien intruder into human nature. Conscience is not a divine voice lodging within the human breast, even though Butler believes most strongly that man has been made in the image of God and that his reason may, in some sense, properly be called 'Divine'. Nor is conscience a kind of separate, tiresome and interfering Jiminy Cricket, something lodged within us but with an existence and identity of its own. D. M. MacKinnon suggests that even Butler's use of the word 'faculty' may be misleading, if we think of it in terms of a 'thing' rather than of a 'capacity': 'It is not that conscience is the name of an esoteric faculty; it is a way of referring to the manner in which human beings comment on their behaviour, and set before themselves the successive tasks and possibilities of their existence.'[4] To reiterate what we said above, for Butler human beings without conscience would hardly be human beings at all. In other words, conscience stands for something in us which is of the very essence of our humanity.

Secondly, Butler wishes to deepen and extend our understanding of what it is to be a human being without taking off into a dreamland of fantasy and superstition. Thus, on the one hand, morality is concerned with happiness and the satisfaction of

[3] Butler, op. cit., p. 287f.
[4] MacKinnon, op. cit., p. 190.

44

human needs and desires. At times he is prepared to talk as if an *enlightened* self-love were all that was required to keep men to the path of morality. On the other hand, self-love must give way to the direction of conscience, which alone has the ultimate authority. It is as if the intuitive judgement of the conscience reveals to us our true selves. In knowing what we ought to do we are acknowledging the claim of what we really are.

It has been objected against Butler that he gives to the intuitive judgements of conscience an ultimacy and an authority which they cannot possibly have. If crimes have been justified in the name of benevolence, they have also been justified in the name of conscience. The intuitive judgements of conscience, it is said, vary from person to person and even from one occasion to another. They themselves need some rigorous scrutiny and appraisal before they can be accepted.

Clearly this is an objection that deserves serious attention. What we must notice here, however, is that Butler's view is not to be identified with the view that the conscience informs us immediately and without reflection what we ought to do, by-passing our inclinations and desires, together with the principles of prudence and benevolence. For Butler conscience is a constitutional monarch, not an autocrat. Its judgements take into account desires and principles. But when these do not of themselves result in a single, agreed decision, then conscience has its part to play. Nor are its judgements arbitrary, even if they are intuitive. For they stem from the conviction that there is a proper order of human nature which determines whether an action is right or wrong, and it is this order which its judgements articulate and express.

We might in this respect compare the judgement of an expert art-dealer who is asked to give his opinion which of two paintings is the original work of a master and which is only a fake. He takes various things into consideration, such as composition, colour, style, brush-work, etc., not all of which point to the same conclusion. He has, then, to weigh one set of considerations against another. This is not an easy or an automatic process. It calls for sensitivity, insight and discrimination. In the end, perhaps, things fall into a definite pattern and his doubts are dispelled. His mind is made up and he gives his opinion. He may even say that he is now certain that he is right in his judgement: one of the two paintings cannot be original, as there is something fundamentally incongruous about it. His judgement, we might say, is, in a sense, intuitive. It is based on a total perception. Nevertheless, it is not arbitrary. It is the result of very careful reflection. The perception is that of a trained mind.

THE VOICE OF GOD

If Butler's view of the workings of the conscience is to be interpreted in some such way as this, even though he would undoubtedly have claimed a greater certainty for the judgement of the conscience than we should be willing to claim for the judgement of the art-dealer, then it is clearly poles apart from any view that seeks to identify the conscience with the voice of God. Butler is not to be counted among those who have claimed direct access to the mind of God, whether in rebellion against an external authority of Scripture or Church, or in accordance with a mystical tradition which has affirmed the existence of a spark of the divine fire at the centre of the human soul.

An appeal to direct and immediate enlightenment has never been generally accepted in the main traditions of the Christian Church. Nevertheless, it is universally agreed that a man ought always to act according to his conscience. Even in those parts of the Church which claim that obedience is due to the highest ecclesiastical authority, since it has been given to that authority to know and to proclaim the will of God, it is at the same time affirmed that a man must not act against his conscience, whatever the bidding of his superiors. If a man acts according to his conscience, he is without sin, even if the Church condemns what he does. If a man acts against his conscience, he commits a sin, even if the Church approves of what he does. Acting according to conscience, however, does not mean that a person should do what he *feels* to be right, instinctively and intuitively. It means that he should do what he *judges* to be right, after he has reflected to the best of his ability according to the canons of practical reason. In circumstances in which he himself has no access to the relevant facts, or in which his own powers of reflection and judgement are limited or impaired, reason itself suggests that he should accept the judgement of the most reliable authority.

Reason, according to this tradition, is God-given. Conscience is not a separate faculty; it is an activity of reason, the application of moral science to conduct. The basic principles of the practical reason are not in dispute. Only in the application of these principles to particular situations is there room for conscientious differences of opinion.

Conscience needs to be informed and instructed; it possesses no guarantee of infallibility. Therefore it is a person's duty to do all in his power to dispel his ignorance. If, having done so, he still believes that it is right for him to act in a way which meets with authority's moral disapproval, then his ignorance is said to be 'invincible' and his action blameless. What he does remains wrong, but he himself is free from fault. Should, however, his ignorance result from some culpable negligence, he is to be blamed, even though he does not think that what he is doing is wrong.

Thomas Aquinas illustrates this point with the following example: 'If a mistaken reason bids a man sleep with another man's wife, to do this will be evil if based on ignorance of a divine law he ought to know; but if the misjudgement is occasioned by thinking that the woman is really his own wife, and she wants him and he wants her, then his will is free from fault.'[5]

Acting according to conscience, then, is no guarantee that a person will thereby do what is morally right. It ensures, at the best, only that a person will be morally blameless. But because it is more important that a person should be morally blameless than that he should do what is actually the right thing to do, conscience maintains for the individual its ultimate authority. Even so, there are limits to what can properly be called a conscientious action. Some moral principles, such as the sanctity of human life, are so fundamental that, if a person openly flouts them, he cannot have begun to reflect morally, even though he pretends to have acted according to conscience. He is an evil man, not a moral nonconformist.

So far we have been thinking in terms of a person's making up his mind conscientiously. In this sense conscience is closely associated with reason. It is primarily concerned with reaching

[5] *Summa Theologica*, 1a 2ae, xix. 6.

a decision about what ought to be done in this or that morally puzzling situation. It is forward-looking. It seeks the good. It is, no doubt, found in association with feeling; but in this case it is an in-formed feeling, a kind of quiet sensitivity rather than a sudden outburst of emotion.

CONSCIENCE AND GUILT

Conscience can, however, be seen in another context and understood in a different way. Here it is very much a matter of feeling, especially of feelings of guilt. It is backward-looking rather than forward-looking and is activated by wrong-doing. It is a kind of moral alarm signal.

Interestingly enough, one of the uses of the word 'conscience' in the New Testament seems to reflect this 'alarm signal' approach. If a man sins, his conscience within him condemns him. If he confesses his sin and is forgiven, then the voice of conscience is silent. Thus a 'good' conscience is a 'silent' conscience. Forgiveness does not intensify the pangs of conscience, it stills them. Or even if feelings of guilt still remain, they are to be disregarded, for 'God is greater than our conscience' (1 John 3.20).

A similarly negative interpretation of conscience is to be found in the psycho-analytic theories of Sigmund Freud (1856–1939).

Freud argued that at the basis of the human psyche are a number of instinctive drives which demand satisfaction in as direct and as immediate a manner as possible. They operate according to what he called the 'pleasure principle'. However, the young child soon discovers that he is living in a world which impedes and restricts his immediate demands and satisfactions. Consequently the pleasure principle has to be adapted to what Freud called the 'reality principle'. Hence the psyche develops a special structure and dynamic to enable it to cope with the harsh realities of life.

The details of Freud's theory cannot be considered now. It is sufficient for our purposes to say that, according to him, the psyche gains some measure of control over its powerful and wayward instincts by turning some of their force back against itself. It creates not only an 'ego', which takes account of the realities of the world and society, but also a 'super-ego', which internalizes and reflects the anger and disapproval of others, not least of the child's father. Thus we arrive at the phenomenon of a 'guilty' conscience, which develops a life and power of its own, irrespective of the deliberate thought and reflection of the individual agent. This 'conscience' is pre-rational, the inevitable outcome of conflict and aggression. (It has been suggested by some that even animals have a 'conscience', or super-ego, of this sort!)

THE 'SUPER-EGO'

The psycho-analytical and the philosophical concepts of conscience must not be confused. They are obviously different from each other. What can be said about the one cannot necessarily be said about the other. We need always to be clear in our own minds, when we are talking about the conscience, which concept we are using. Butler's concept of the conscience, for example, is clearly closer to Freud's 'ego' than to his 'super-ego', since it is very much the attempt of reason to order the basic inclinations and desires according to the realities of man and the world. Indeed, it is interesting to note that some psychologists since Freud have suggested a fundamental revision of his basically mechanistic and deterministic dynamics, and have moved the emphasis away from the pre-rational control of the 'super-ego' and have placed it on the adaptive and integrating function of the 'ego'. In this theory the 'mature and healthy' conscience is to be identified with the 'ego's' reflection on the best way of achieving integrity and community, while the 'immature and pathological' conscience is to be identified with the mass of feelings of guilt which have been imbibed at an early and pre-rational age from a demanding parent. These two 'consciences' may come into conflict. I may, for example, still *feel* guilty about playing tennis on a Sunday, because it was once instilled into me that Sunday was not the right day for fun and games, although now I no longer *believe* that it is wrong to play games on a Sunday.

An interesting comparison between the 'super-ego' and the mature conscience has been made by John Glaser.[6] The 'super-

[6] See *Theological Studies*, vol. 32 (1971), pp. 30–47. Reprinted in C. Ellis Nelson, ed., *Conscience*. Newman Press 1973.

ego' commands that an act be performed in order to gain approval. It is more concerned with its own feelings than with the objective of the action. It is static and fixed. It blindly 'obeys' an acknowledged authority. It responds to actions taken out of context. It is more concerned with the past than with the future. It swings from feelings of guilt to feelings of self-satisfaction, and the guilt it feels bears little relation to the actual moral quality of the action. The mature conscience, on the other hand, calls for action in order to create something of value. It is outward-looking rather than inward-looking. It is dynamic, responsible and responsive. It develops in insight as each new situation presents itself. It is concerned with the rights and wrongs of a situation rather than with the commands of an overwhelming authority. It interprets actions in their larger context and significance. It looks to the future rather than to the past. It acknowledges guilt where responsibility has been misused, but at the same time looks forward in expectation of an increased sensitivity and a more discerning response.

The 'super-ego', then, is a mechanism which reflects man's social nature. He belongs to a group. His own life depends in part on the relations which he establishes with other members of his group. The group imposes some restriction and control on the satisfaction of his private desires. In this way a measure of harmony and co-operation can be achieved. Society can survive.

The conscience, on the other hand, is the expression of the individual's own search for self-direction and self-fulfilment. It claims an autonomy over against social pressures. The individual person is not content to be one of the crowd and to do just what everybody else does. He makes his own judgements of good and bad, right and wrong. He demands freedom of conscience for himself and for everyone else.

INDIVIDUAL AND SOCIETY

There is here a potential source of conflict between the individual and society. If and when such a conflict occurs, which is to give way to the other?

From one point of view there seems to be an obvious answer

to this question. Surely the whole is greater, and therefore more important, than the part? If one thinks of society as a kind of organism, with a life and identity of its own, individuals may be seen as organs, or parts, of society as a whole. Sometimes a part has to be sacrificed for the well-being of the whole. It may be necessary to remove a troublesome tooth, or a diseased limb, for the good of the whole body. So the individual must give way to the will of the majority, for the majority represents the will of the people. The people's welfare has the first priority. There is an old Latin tag: *salus populi, prima lex* (the safety of the people is the first law).

This argument has a certain plausibility. In times of national crisis it has something of importance to say. On the other hand, it has been used to justify the most autocratic of regimes and the suppression of individual liberties. Society is not an organism, because it possesses no single centre of consciousness, as does an individual human being. Nor can ideas of a healthy body be transferred to yield parallel ideas of a healthy society. Sometimes it may be the case that society is sick, and that the individual's protest against society is a symptom of health rather than of illness. If he were 'well-adjusted' to society, he would be as sick as the society itself.

So the individual asserts the freedom of his own conscience. But what is it about an individual's own conscience which gives it, in the eyes of many, a distinctive and supreme importance? By what right does the individual stand over against society? What is it that is so special about the individual and his conscience that we must pay it special regard and respect?

THE IMPORTANCE OF PERSONS

The short answer to this question, I suggest, is that we are convinced that *persons matter*. By 'persons' we mean individual human beings who not only have such and such experiences, but who also have it in their power to interpret and respond to these experiences. Persons, that is, are agents. They can make their own decisions. To some extent they are authors of their own actions. They do not merely react to external stimuli, they respond freely. The value of the individual conscience, then, is

51

bound up with the value that we place on persons who respond freely with their own decisions. If they are only the organs of society, they are less than persons.

What is it, however, that makes a person's free decision *his* decision? Is it simply that *he* decides rather than have the decision made for him by somebody else? Would this not be compatible with a highly arbitrary decision, say, with tossing a coin? Is this the much vaunted individual freedom which is at the root of the regard which we are supposed to pay to the individual conscience?

It is not simply the freedom of choice which makes a decision peculiarly a person's own decision, it is also the rationality, or reflectiveness, of the choice. It must be a considered choice rather than a passing whim. It must reflect his deepest beliefs, those with which he identifies himself. He has given it thought.

A conscientious decision, then, is a personal decision which expresses a judgement which an individual can reject only at the cost of rejecting himself. Many of our decisions are, no doubt, free and considered; but not all of them involve our deepest selves. Where they do, there we may perhaps speak of the conscience and ascribe to it a fundamental and supreme authority.

At this stage of our discussion we are still seeking the source of conscience's authority within the individual himself. We have gone beyond the mere fact of a free decision and we have brought into focus the fundamental values by which a person lives, those with which he identifies himself. These are his supreme 'goods', what he really approves and what he really wants, what he believes that others too would really approve and want if they had the insight and understanding which he has acquired. A matter of conscience is a matter which touches upon the deep, fundamental and human concerns of the individual.

HUMAN NATURE

We have, then, in this description of the authority of the conscience recognized the formal requirements of morality, namely, prescriptivity, authority and logical impartiality. But are we left with the view that the individual is ultimately a moral law unto himself? Has conscience no authority *over* the individual's

52

desires, including his deep desires? What if the deep desires of one individual differ from those of another? What has happened to the imperious command of conscience? Has its imperative been reduced to a hypothetical: *if* you really want so-and-so, *then* you must do so-and-so? Is the individual subject to no claim outside himself, whether that claim is the claim of society, or the claim of humanity, or the claim of a moral law independent of human desires, or the claim of an ultimate order of things which he is called to respect, whether this order is personal or impersonal?

It must surely be admitted that we sometimes do not want to do what we recognize that we ought to do. If we are to say that on such occasions we *really* want to do what we ought to do, and that it is only our disordered desires which tempt us away from doing what we really want to do, then we must face the question how we are to discover what we really want to do. And if the answer is given that we discover what we really want to do by deciding what we ought to do, then we are arguing in a circle. We get our 'ought' from our 'really want' and our 'really want' from our 'ought'.

We find ourselves coming back to the question which Butler raised for us. Rationality prompts us to an enlightened self-interest. Benevolence prompts us to make the concerns of others our own concerns. When these principles conflict, as sometimes they undoubtedly do, how is the conflict to be settled? By the conscience, says Butler; for it is the conscience that discerns the ultimate moral order and mediates its authoritative claim.

But how are we to articulate this order and this claim? If Butler was mistaken in locating it in the intuitive responses to particular situations, can we locate it somewhere else? Do we, for example, recognize some values as mandatory rather than optional, so that we are bound to acknowledge their authority over us, even if we cannot be sure how these values are to be expressed in any particular action? Can we give any more thorough account than that which Butler provides of the order of human nature which establishes the criterion for right and wrong actions?

At this point we are moving on from considerations of individual self-interest and social harmony to considerations which have a metaphysical flavour about them. If we wish to do justice to our specifically human existence, must we recognize in human nature, not only its present inclinations and desires, hopes and longings, but also what it has within it to become? Does conscience witness to the fact that our human nature, though rooted in the past and given to us with its inheritance of instincts, desires and interests, is not completely fixed and given? We are challenged to enter the realm of freedom and responsibility. We must decide for ourselves what it is that we are to become. Our potentialities are as important a part of our human nature as our actualities. We may speak metaphorically of the call of the future, the challenge of the 'not yet'. Or we may speak in overtly religious terms of the call and command of God. Does the 'voice' of conscience remind us that we are responsible for what, in our decisions, we have made of ourselves and also for what we shall make of ourselves?

If this line of thought has anything in it which is worth further exploration, then the significance of the conscience is to be found not only in the integrity of its own fundamental values, but also in its witness to a bond between man and man, and between the past, the present and the future. It is a witness to the importance of community and continuity, to the interdependence of freedom and belonging. A man's life is his own and yet it is not his own.

Here we are moving up to and beyond the frontiers of morality. We are opening windows on to fundamental beliefs concerning man and his status in the world. We are asking questions which are also the concern of religion. Before we go further in this direction, however, let us ask ourselves: What is the point of morality? The question itself, as well as some of the answers which we shall be considering, takes us over similar ground to that which we have already been exploring. It is possible, however, that the landscape will become clearer as we approach it now from a slightly different direction.

DISCUSSION QUESTIONS

In the following syllogism the conclusion follows logically from the premisses. The premisses both seem plausible; yet the conclusion seems paradoxical. Why is this?

It is always right to do what you believe to be right.
What you believe to be right is sometimes wrong.
Therefore it is sometimes right to do what is wrong.

Is a man morally blameless for killing women and children if he honestly believes that such acts are necessary in the cause of liberation?

How does one distinguish between a 'terrorist' and a 'freedom-fighter'?

5

WHY BE MORAL?

Why should I do my duty? Why should I do what I ought to do when it causes me pain and distress?

Some philosophers have argued that there is no answer to this question. This is not because they have looked for an answer and have failed to find one. It is because the question is not a proper question. It sounds as if it makes sense, but in fact it doesn't. It is rather like asking why a square has four sides. But a four-sided figure is just what a square is. So, it is said, my duty, or what I ought to do, is just what I should do. Get clear in your mind what you mean by your duty and you won't ask such a silly question again.

We can make the same point in another way. Any reason which may be offered for doing what one ought to do will appeal either to moral considerations or to non-moral considerations. If it appeals to moral considerations, the same question crops up again: Why should I take any notice of these considerations? If it appeals to non-moral considerations, such as, for example, bribes and threats, then the moral point of view has been abandoned for a non-moral, probably a prudential, point of view. Morality has not been justified, it has been argued out of existence. The point of view has changed and something other than morality has taken the stage. So, it is asserted, morality must be self-justifying. The only necessary and sufficient reason for doing what is morally right is the fact that it is morally right.

This sounds plausible. Suppose, for example, we commend honesty as a moral virtue, and then someone comes along and asks why he should be honest. We may reply: 'Because honesty is the best policy.' This is a non-moral attempt at justification. It appeals to self-interest. It implies that, if honesty did not pay, there would be no need to be honest. Now many people are dishonest because they believe that, when it comes to hard facts, dishonesty pays. If honesty is a *moral* principle, does it not mean that we ought to be honest, whether it pays us or not? So, it is argued, morality stands on its own feet. It does not require any external support.

THE POINT OF MORALITY

At this stage, however, we may begin to hesitate. Is being moral really self-justifying, like making music or making friends? If someone were to ask us what we found of real value and interest, and we answered 'Having fun', he would understand us, even if he disapproved of our frivolity. But if we answered 'Being moral and doing our duty', even if he approved of our seriousness, would he really understand us? Must not morality have some point beyond itself?

It has been suggested that morality, with its concepts of right, duty, obligation and virtue, has in fact a point. It serves a definite purpose. It relates in some way to human fulfilment, with which are associated the different but not unconnected concepts of desire, need, interest, benefit, harm, etc. Morality, it is said, can be justified in terms of human 'flourishing'.

In order to avoid the objection that such a justification of morality reduces morality to something other than itself, the following analogy can be used. Morality is like a game—no doubt a very serious game. Within the game certain rules operate. They make the game what it is. In terms of the game these rules are final and decisive.

In a game of football a player may be penalized. If he asks what he has done wrong, the referee may reply that he was offside. If the player admits that he was offside, but argues that he should not have been penalized, because the crowd had come to see him score a goal, the referee can only say that this fact is utterly irrelevant to the game, and that he and all the players are bound by the rules. If the player does not like the rules, then he can leave the field and give up football; but as long as he wants to go on playing he must obey the rules. So it is now up to the player to make up his mind whether he wants to go on playing or not.

57

Might one make a similar move in the case of morality? Within the moral system moral considerations and moral rules are ultimate and decisive. But is it not open to an individual to ask why he should place himself within the moral system, or, in the language that we have been using, why he should play the moral game? 'What is the point of morality?' seems to make sense, even if 'Why should I do my duty?' makes no sense.

G. J. Warnock has suggested that the point of morality is that it is one method of alleviating what he calls 'the human predicament'.

> The 'general object' of morality ... is to contribute to betterment—or non-deterioration—of the human predicament, primarily and essentially by seeking to countervail 'limited sympathies' and their potentially most damaging effects. It is the proper business of morality ... not of course to add to our available resources, nor—directly anyway—to our knowledge of how to make advantageous use of them, nor—again, not directly—to make us more rational in the judicious pursuit of our interests and ends; its proper business is to expand our sympathies, or, better, to reduce the liability to damage inherent in their natural tendency to be narrowly restricted.[1]

Men need one another and depend on one another; but their lack of sympathy and concern for one another often results in disharmony and conflict, so that the interests of all are damaged. Moral rules and moral virtues 'countervail' this tendency towards general deterioration. Both the cultivation of moral virtues, such as benevolence, honesty and fairness, and the formulation of moral principles and practices, such as those of equality before the law and the care of the aged and infirm, have their rationale in the human predicament. Morality shapes character and action in such a way that men may better live at peace with one another and further the common good. The moral order is an order that stems from a fundamental human need. Its general outlines can be filled in, its details will depend on time and circumstance.

---

[1] G. J. Warnock, *The Object of Morality* (Methuen 1971), p. 26.

If such is the object of morality, why should I be moral? War-nock's answer to this question is not that it is somehow irrational to reject morality, but that I may come to *want* to be moral because I want what morality is intended to achieve. 'It is possible for one to want human predicaments to be in general amelio-rated, and thus to feel as practically efficacious that range of reasons which has that ultimate *rationale.*'[2]

If I want what morality is intended to achieve, and believe that morality is an effective means towards securing that end, then I have the very best of reasons for being moral. But what is to be said if I do not want the betterment of the human condi-tion, if I am more or less indifferent to the fate of my fellow human beings? How can I be persuaded to care if I do not really care? And what am I to make of it if I am told that I *ought* to care?

Argument at this point is limited in what it can hope to achieve. Argument is concerned primarily with bringing to light errors in reasoning. But wants are desires, and when it comes to our desires reason plays only a subordinate role.

It is possible that I may be confused, and so inconsistent, about what I want. Argument may help me to dispel this con-fusion and to discover that my real wants, of which I had not been fully conscious, are different from what I had believed. I may discover that deep down I do care about other human beings passionately, and that I had assumed a mask of selfish-ness only to protect my emotional vulnerability. Alternatively, I may discover that deep down I am much more selfish than I had believed, and that my apparent concern for others was only a mask which I wore in order to appear respectable. Argu-ment may be one of the means of acquiring self-knowledge. However, it is not the only means, and its power is often minimal. Something else is required to bring me to recognize the truth of what I really am and what I really want.

---

[2] Ibid., p. 165.

Alternatively, argument may take as its premiss the assumption that my basic want is my own happiness. It may assume that, even if I am not concerned about others, I am concerned about myself. So an appeal is made to self-interest. How successful can such an appeal be?

If I want to achieve my own desires, more likely than not I shall need the help and co-operation of others. Therefore I need to learn the basic rules on which co-operation can be based. I must give at least some attention to what others are trying to achieve in co-operation with me. I must play the moral game.

Considerations such as these may lead me some way towards observing the principles of morality. But they are notoriously unreliable. If I think I can get away without observing the rules, or if I think I am in such a strong position that I can afford to ignore the moral rules, then the argument that being moral is to my own advantage falls to the ground. It is certainly to my advantage that other people observe the rules; but it is far from evident that it is to my advantage that here and now I observe the rules. Unbridled selfishness suggests that I pay some regard to morality, but not too much.

The fundamental weakness of this appeal to self-interest is that, by making the welfare of others an instrument to my own welfare, it abandons the moral point of view. Morality makes good sense if what I want, *for its own sake and not for the sake of something else*, is the welfare of others. It does not make good sense, though the outward observance of moral rules may make some sense, if I do not want for its own sake the welfare of others.

So we return to people's fundamental wants. Is there any way in which we can persuade people to want the goals which morality subserves? The moral teacher cannot rest content with instructing his pupils in the processes of moral reasoning; he must also endeavour to communicate to them his own sense that the goals of morality are intrinsically worthwhile.

Readiness to think and act from the moral point of view is dependent upon the ability to feel and see things from a moral point of view. It is necessary that a person should be able to identify himself with others, to put himself in somebody else's shoes. Thus moral education must concern itself with the imagination and the feelings as much as with reason and argument.

This process of identification with others has a natural basis. A member of a family or a group finds himself identifying with the other members. A child may identify with his mother or his father. An adolescent may identify with another adolescent in his peer-group. These natural processes, however, have their limitations. They go hand in hand with equally natural processes whereby a person wishes to distinguish himself from others, to discover his own individual identity, sometimes in contrast and opposition to others. There is a natural process of exclusion as well as of inclusion. I can feel very strongly that I am a member of a group because I can compare myself with someone else who is not a member of the group. The existence of the outsider contributes to the solidarity of the insiders. Consequently the process of identifying with others may lead to a kind of extended egoism rather than to a direct concern with others in themselves. If there is to develop a direct concern for others a person must be prepared to 'lose' himself for the sake of others.

There is no need to assume that human beings are by nature never anything but selfish. It is not impossible to hold that there are certain natural sentiments of humanity which make people want to alleviate the suffering of others. 'Wanting', as such, is not necessarily selfish. I may want other people to be happy more than I want my own happiness. Even so, one has to admit that these sentiments of humanity, even if they exist, jostle with all sorts of other feelings and sentiments. They are not naturally dominant. If people are to be persuaded to adopt a moral point of view, sentiments of humanity must somehow be supported and strengthened, to say the very least. Man may not be incurably and irredeemably selfish; nevertheless his selfishness runs very deep.

BELONGING

What seems to be needed, if the moral point of view is to hold a man's attention and allegiance, is some kind of ex-centering, whereby the centre of his world is no longer himself and his own individual needs and satisfactions, but a family of mankind to which he himself belongs along with others and within which the welfare of each becomes the welfare of all.

There are various visions of this kind, some religious, some non-religious; but at the heart of them all is the conviction that in some way men belong to one another, and that beneath the conflicts of individual with individual, group with group, there is some sort of essential unity demanding to be realized. Such a vision finds classic expression in the words of John Donne:

> No man is an Iland, intire of it selfe; every man is a peece of the Continent, a part of the maine; if a Clod bee washed away by the Sea, Europe is the lesse, as well as if a Promontorie were, as well as if a Mannor of thy friends or of thine owne were; any mans death diminishes me, because I am involved in Mankinde; And therefore never send to know for whom the bell tolls; It tolls for thee.[3]

What are the status and function of visions such as this? That they have the power to shape and focus the way in which we see our life in the world, to engage our deepest feelings and to determine our basic attitudes, is undeniable. Men have lived and died in following a vision. But can we say more than that they are products of the imagination, that they act as a spur for some but not for others, that they are stories which some men like to tell in order to give them added incentive to pursue a path of action which they have decided to pursue on other grounds? In short, are these visions pictures in the fire, or do they give us some insight into a reality to which otherwise we should have

[3] From *Devotions upon Emergent Occasions*, XVII.

been blind? If they are only pictures in the fire, then they cannot give us a reason to be moral. If, however, they are windows into 'ultimate reality', then it is possible that an appeal to such a vision may indeed give me a reason for being moral. What sort of reason?

The sort of reason, whether it is religious or non-religious, is expressed metaphorically by the affirmation that morality goes with the grain of the universe. Individual and social life are part of a larger pattern. They find their origin and fulfilment in that larger pattern. The fundamental nature of human beings accords with the ultimate nature of things. Even though they are free to act against this pattern and nature, there is something self-defeating about such action.

It is characteristic of all such arguments that appearances must not be taken at their face value. Things are not altogether what they seem. There is a surface level for human life and there is also a deep level. Reality is such that one needs to have one's eyes opened to ultimate patterns and structures. In terms of these patterns and structures morality and the object of morality make sense.

One way of putting the point is to say that *in the end* duty and interest coincide. It may even be asserted, although this will probably fail to carry conviction, that even in this life the greatest happiness is achieved by doing what is right, that virtue is its own reward. Here and now interest seems too often to pull one way and duty another. But what if we place the 'here and now' in the context of eternity? We recall that even Kant, who distinguished duty sharply from happiness, and argued that a man must do what is right simply because it is right and not because of any satisfaction that he might get out of it, felt bound to postulate the existence of an omnipotent God whose function was to ensure that *in the end* virtue should receive that reward of happiness which it deserved.

It sounds very much as if the argument is in the last analysis being reduced to one of prudence, that if you take eternity as well as time into account, morality does in fact pay off. That crude arguments of this sort are sometimes put forward, not least in religion, we have to admit. But the argument is not intended to operate at this crude level. One could say that a person

63

will not find his true happiness until he has learned to stop thinking about his own happiness. He must become a different person from what he is at present. Or one could say that a person may come to believe that his own happiness really does not matter, that he is willing even to be damned if thereby others may be saved. It is his 'pleasure' to deny himself for the sake of others.

If a person is asked why he is moral, he may reply that he wants to be moral. If the questioner cannot imagine why anyone should want to be moral, he may just accept the fact that different people want different things, some of them very odd at that. But if he is willing to be convinced that it might make good sense to want to be moral, then he may have to be patient enough to listen to an account of what life is really about and how morality fits in with this total picture. The debate is no longer about morality in isolation; it is about metaphysics, or religion. If their claim to be making true assertions about matters of fact can be upheld—even though the 'fact' is not such as can be verified by the empirical sciences or by common-sense observation—then they clearly have something to say about the basis of morality and perhaps also about its content. So we turn from questions of duty to questions of salvation, from morality to religion.

DISCUSSION QUESTIONS

Is my wanting to do something a good reason for my doing it, or is it no reason at all? Might my wanting to do it itself be unreasonable? If so, in what sense?

'Virtue is its own reward.' 'You will never be happy unless you are good.' Consider the different ways in which people have tried to bring together the ideas of virtue and of happiness. Which do you find plausible?

Does the imagination provide insight into reality or escape from reality?

6

MORALITY AND RELIGION: CONFLICT

We began our analysis of morality without making any reference to religion. We found ourselves using the language of right and wrong, good and bad, principles and virtues. These were words and ideas which would have been the common currency of anyone seriously concerned to reflect on the ways in which human beings ought to behave and the kind of persons that they ought to be, whether he himself was religiously minded or not. In tracing the geography of these concepts we raised basic questions about human nature, individual freedom and the restraints needed by any society if it is not to disintegrate when the interests of its members conflict.

Only occasionally did we make any reference to religion. At the end of the last chapter we suggested that there might be a religious answer to the question why anyone should want to be moral. Religion might exercise a co-ordinating and integrating function by holding before men's eyes the vision of an ultimate universal order in which the needs of the individual and the needs of humanity were harmonized. It could bind human beings to one another by binding them all to something even more inclusive, whether this were conceived in terms of an impersonal order or in terms of a personal God.

The insulation of morality from religion, the demarcation of boundaries which each must observe, makes good sense for an increasingly large number of people today. It should be remembered, however, how strange this procedure would have seemed to others in different societies and earlier ages.

In most traditional societies religious beliefs, social institutions and individual ideals would have formed something of an organic whole. The sacred and the secular interpenetrated. Indeed, the distinction itself as we understand it is a modern phenomenon. Individuals understood themselves in terms of their social status and society's practices were validated by religious belief and ritual. It would have made no sense to distinguish sharply between morality and religion, since morality was religious through and through, as regards both its contents and its sanctions.

In some societies, in which religion still plays an important integrating function, the union of religion and morality is unbroken. In many societies, however, there has been a divorce. The process of breakdown has been gradual, and there is no single convincing reason to explain why it has occurred. Sociologists often refer to a process of secularization, and Peter Berger defines this as follows: 'By secularization we mean the process by which sectors of society and culture are removed from the domination of religious institutions and symbols.'[1] This process affects both the structure of society and the consciousness of individuals. Institutions become independent of each other and establish their own rules and regulations. Individuals interpret life in non-religious ways. Religious beliefs lose their plausibility and no longer serve to provide a single and cohesive moral pattern. Instead, individuals and groups fashion their own ideals and society is held together by a minimal morality which is sufficient to make life in society possible. To draw an analogy, there must be a rule of the road to keep traffic flowing and to prevent as many accidents as possible; but it is up to each driver to decide for himself where and when he will travel. So it is that in most Western industrialized countries Church and society have lost their identity, religion has become more and more a private affair, and morality has become secular.[2]

In this chapter we shall be looking at some of the criticisms which upholders of religious and secular morality have levelled at each other. In the following chapter we shall consider whether there is any common ground on which they can all agree.

Religious people are often heard to assert that morality cannot survive for long without the support of religion. When

[1] P. L. Berger, *The Social Reality of Religion* (Faber & Faber 1969), p. 107.

[2] By a 'secular' morality I mean a non-religious morality. It is sometimes called a natural, or a rational, morality. However, it is questionable whether a religious morality is either unnatural or non-rational.

people cease to be religious, they cease to be moral. It is religion which validates moral beliefs and undergirds moral attitudes. The moral law has no authority over anyone if it is only a man-made law. If man has made the law, he is just as capable of un-making it. If, on the other hand, the moral law stems from a divine law-giver, then it has an authority which is more than human and which it behoves men to obey. Furthermore, as a divine law-giver, God may be expected to enforce his law with divine sanctions. If men obey the divine law, they may hope for eternal life; but if they flout the divine law, they may expect eternal damnation. What could provide a stronger motive than that for keeping within the bounds of the moral law?

THE SECULARIST ARGUMENT

Secular moralists reject both the theory and the practice. Let us consider the practice first.

In the name of religion, it is said, all sorts of moral atrocities have been committed. In crusade and holy war men have fought and killed in order to glorify their God. They have tortured in order to compel heretics to confess the 'true' faith. They have conquered and enslaved, suppressed liberty and prevented in-quiry. If the history of religiously inspired behaviour is to be fully chronicled, it will turn out to be a history of cruelty and corruption.

Furthermore, the hope of heaven and the fear of hell have no beneficial effect on men's behaviour. In reply to Cleanthes' last-ditch argument that 'the doctrine of a future state is so strong and necessary a security to morals, that we never ought to abandon or neglect it', David Hume (1711–76) makes Philo reply:

It is certain, from experience, that the smallest grain of natural honesty and benevolence has more effect on men's conduct, than the most pompous views suggested by theological theories and systems. A man's natural inclination works in-cessantly upon him ... Whereas religious motives, where they act at all, operate only by starts and bounds.[3]

[3] 'Dialogues Concerning Natural Religion', in Richard Wollheim, ed., *Hume on Religion* (Fontana 1963), p. 196f.

Religious sanctions have little or no effect. Were it otherwise, divines would hardly have to berate their flocks for their wickedness and sin!

If the days of religious cruelty and intolerance are now mostly past, the argument continues, this is not the result of the teaching of religion. Men have grown weary of religious bigotry. They have learned the virtue of tolerance because they have become impatient of religious enthusiasm, not because they have become enthusiastically religious. It is a secular morality that has been the instrument of peace.

Lastly, even if it is now true of religious believers that they share with their unbelieving fellows most of the same values, including a respect for liberty of conscience, nevertheless they are often busy about their religious duties when they ought to be busy about their moral duties. The other-worldliness of religion with its emphasis on individual salvation draws a man away from the responsibilities which this world lays upon him.

So much for some of the charges which the secularist levels against religious people's moral practice. Now let us listen to their objections against the theory underlying religious morality.

First, consider the matter of religious sanctions. If the fundamental motivation for behaving morally is the fear of what will happen to oneself if one behaves immorally, then self-interest of the most blatant kind has been built into the foundations of the religious life.

Now some philosophers find nothing objectionable in the belief that obedience is owed to God because he is omnipotent, and therefore disobedience is the height of irrationality. The fear of the Lord is the beginning of wisdom, though it is not the whole of wisdom. Others, however, find this belief morally repulsive. A modern philosopher, for example, can write: 'If my first and chief reason for worshipping God had to be a belief that a super-Frankenstein would blast me to hell if I did not, then I hope I should have the decency to tell this being, who is named Almighty God, to go ahead and blast.'[4]

Secondly, how is the love of God supposed to be related to the love of neighbour? Presumably the religious believer should

[4] Rush Rhees, *Without Answers* (Routledge and Kegan Paul 1969), p. 113.

do everything that he does for God's sake. In that case, he must love his neighbour for God's sake. But this converts the love of neighbour into a means of loving and glorifying God. Human beings are treated as means and not as ends in themselves. In secular morality, on the other hand, where there is no God demanding that we love him with all our heart and mind, human beings can be treated as ends in themselves and loved for their own sakes.

This brings us to the third and final objection to which we must give attention. It is probably the most important objection of all.

Religious morality, it is said, is based on obedience to God, whereas secular morality is based on human freedom and responsibility. If obedience is taken to be the fundamental concept of morality, then the proper autonomy of morality is lost.

> We must never lose sight of the distinction between what we are told to do and what we ought to do. There is a point beyond which we cannot get rid of our own moral responsibilities by laying them on the shoulders of a superior, whether he be general, priest or politician, human or divine. Anyone who thinks otherwise has not understood what a moral decision is.[5]

The morally responsible person has to make up his own mind what he ought to do. It must be his action and not another's. Religious morality keeps men in a state of childhood and subservience. They are not allowed to question. The Lord God has commanded—and that is that.

Furthermore, just as the responsible moral agent must assert his proper autonomy, so too must the standards that he recognizes have their proper autonomy. They exercise a claim upon him in their own right. Their authority is intrinsic to themselves. If, for example, a man does not recognize the moral claim of other human beings upon his consideration and regard, then he does not understand what a moral claim is. If he observes an act of wanton cruelty and sees nothing in it to condemn, until he has been told that God has condemned such actions, then

[5] R. M. Hare, *Applications of Moral Philosophy* (Macmillan 1972), p. 8.

69

he is morally blind. Wanton cruelty is morally wrong, God or no God. It offends against the moral law. This law is 'autonomous' in the sense that its validity is independent of religion. It does not first acquire validity because it has been promulgated by Almighty God.

Secular moralists have posed the following question to anyone who believes that the authority of the moral law derives from the fact that it has been decreed by God. Is something morally right because God commands it; or does God command it because it is morally right?[6] If the religious moralist replies that it is morally right because God commands it, then it follows that anything would be right if God commanded it. If God commanded Abraham to slay Isaac, or Hitler to exterminate the Jews, it would still be right. But surely that is preposterous. If, however, the religious moralist replies that God commands it because it is morally right, then the moral law is independent of God's will and we need not concern ourselves further with what God commands or does not command. God himself is bound by the moral law.

Confronted with this dilemma, religious thinkers are, on the whole, unwilling to think of God either as arbitrarily willing this rather than that or as subject to a law more ultimate than himself. An arbitrary God would be unworthy of worship, while a God subject to a moral law not of his own making would not be Almighty God. They argue, therefore, that God does not just happen to will this or that, as if he were tossing a coin. What he wills stems from what he is. Being the God he is, his will is indeflectibly directed towards the well-being of his creatures. Hence the dilemma can be escaped. Furthermore, it is asked, if one is going to talk of a moral law, or of values that command our acknowledgement, what sort of reality is to be attributed to this law or to these values? In ordinary language laws and values exist in relation to personal beings who think and choose and act. Does it not make good sense, then, to think of the moral law or of mandatory values in relation to a divine personal being, grounded in his will?

This debate continues. The main question, however, still re-

[6] An early version of this dilemma is to be found in Plato's dialogue *Euthyphro*.

70

mains. If God is God, can he leave any *room* in his universe for man's moral freedom and responsibility? Is it not swallowed up in obedience to God?

THE RELIGIOUS ARGUMENT

The firing is not all from one side. Religious believers make a counter-attack. They have their own objections to make to what they sometimes call 'mere' morality, that is, morality which claims to be securely grounded in individual freedom and social need, without any religious context or backing.

They do not deny that the record of religion is stained with blood, or that religion has been used by evil men to validate their evil ways. Nor do they wish to assert that, if a man is non-religious, he must also be a bad man. They recognize both the saints of belief and the 'saints' of unbelief. The facts are what they are, complex, ambiguous and open to more than one possible explanation.

The heart of their complaint is that secular morality has within it the seeds of its own destruction. It claims to be a rational morality, but rationality cannot bridge the gap between my interests and the interests of my fellow men. It claims to be a natural morality, but human nature, being what it is, can provide only shifting sands on which to build a stable and universal morality.

The appeal to rationality in place of revelation has its attraction. Rationality sounds as if it would be something of which everyone approved and concerning which everyone would be agreed, whereas the claim to have been vouchsafed a revelation, in whatever shape or form, is disputable and disputed. But is rationality anything other than consistency? And would not most people say that a person was acting rationally when he was motivated by enlightened self-love? Enlightened self-love does no doubt engender some sort of moral system. If human beings cannot be certain to what extent they will be able to achieve their own ends without the co-operation, or at least the non-interference, of others, then it is rational to agree on some basic rules of social behaviour. Some standards of fairness make sense, so that no one's interests will be trampled over simply because

71

through weakness or mischance he finds himself suddenly at the bottom of the pecking order. Nevertheless, as we have already had occasion to observe, a moral system which is based on the rationality of self-interest is limited in its comprehensiveness and liable to break down when self-interest calls the tune.

A moral system like this is of limited power just because its fundamental principle is that of fairness. Fairness itself is open to a number of interpretations. It could mean, it is true, that everyone should have equal opportunity to satisfy his needs and to develop his potentialities. In this sense fairness comes very close to loving one's neighbour as oneself. But it is more likely to mean insisting on one's own rights. For the open conflict between individual and individual is substituted a kind of moral conflict. Everyone pursues his own interests, not now by brute force, but by demanding his rights, and by making these rights as extensive as possible. Of course, the notion of a right is a notion that applies to others as well as to oneself. That is, rights involve duties. But this aspect of fairness tends all too easily to be forgotten. Whether it is forgotten or not, it can hardly be denied that a society that lives only in terms of rights and duties is unlikely to generate unselfishness, sacrifice and love. A family, for example, which made fairness its supreme principle is hardly likely to flourish. 'If he doesn't do his share of the work, why should I do mine?' is a question which is hardly likely to foster family life.

If love of one's neighbour is, as many religious and non-religious people believe, the supreme moral virtue, the demands of love must be admitted to exceed the demands of fairness, for fairness is based on defined and limited expectations, while love, at least in principle, acknowledges no limits. This difference between a morality of fairness and a morality of love is stressed by Helen Oppenheimer when she contrasts what Christians profess with what they actually believe:

What we nearly all really believe in, deeply and even passionately, whether we realize it or not, is *fairness*, and whatever we say or think we believe about Christianity, when it comes to the test it is generally fairness that prevails. Much as we admire the idea of turning the other cheek, we are reluctant to teach it to our children of school age: it would be terribly hard on them. Much as we approve of loving one's enemies, we really mind if a villain gets away with it: that would be really too bad. Much as we should like to forgive those who trespass against us, we feel that we can hardly be expected to go on taking trouble over people who continually fail to appreciate our efforts: that is just quixotic ... These are realities on which Christian and non-Christian tacitly agree; any one who denies them is not thought extra good but extra foolish.[7]

Fairness, no doubt, is rational. But is fairness enough? Can it even be *really fair*, once we go below the surface of men's behaviour and take into account their individuality with its subtle variation of insight, capacity, character and need? Do we not require, as religion suggests, either to transform morality or to go beyond morality?

If rationality provides no solid foundation for morality, neither does human nature. For morality requires that people should want the betterment of the human condition, even more than they want the betterment of their own condition. But, left to themselves, people do not want this. They are caught up in the mesh of their own selfish desires. Their own nature is disordered. It needs a radical reordering. Thus what religion demands and offers is salvation. Religious morality is based on the need and possibility of such salvation. Neither nature nor rationality can solve man's conflicts. Religion offers the only sure hope.

Thus the *rationale* of a religious morality is the conviction that man's fundamental need is to be saved from himself. Religious morality does not stem from a rational attempt to harmonize men's conflicting interests, to hold the ring and to ensure that the fight is fairly fought. This attempt is bound to fail because each individual is left to pursue his own desires and to seek his own satisfaction, even though moral restrictions are imposed in order to eliminate 'unfair practices'. The root problem of man's desires as such is not tackled at all. Men themselves are taken

[7] Helen Oppenheimer, *The Character of Christian Morality* (Faith Press 1965), p. 21.

to be the best judges of their own interests. But they are not, for they are blinded by ignorance and sin. They need enlightenment and renewal. Religion goes behind appearances and penetrates to the heart of the human predicament. Here the one question that cries aloud for an answer is 'What must I do to be saved?'

Different religions give different answers to this question, all of them involving both a reorientation of insight and understanding and a new pattern of action. One tradition of Hinduism, for example, claims that man's fundamental error is his imagining that the world of sense experience is the real world, when in fact the real world is the world of the Absolute self with which his own deep self is identical. Thus insight into reality will free a man from the bondage to illusion. Again, Theravāda Buddhism emphasizes a particular discipline and practice. It is desires as such which are the source of man's sickness. He must learn the way of non-attachment, become un-self-ish and so discover the path that leads to final and complete liberation. Again, Christianity affirms that man's troubles stem from his disobedience to God. It is not so much ignorance as sin that is the flaw in human nature. Man knows in his heart of hearts that he owes allegiance to his Creator, but he chooses disobedience. Salvation must include repentance and reconciliation.

The Christian tradition often stresses that a consequence of man's disobedience is that he is no longer able in his own strength to act morally. His religious disobedience has resulted in moral weakness, if not moral impotence. Despite the much vaunted autonomy of the moral agent, experience shows that a man very often knows what he ought to do but is unable to do it. The experience of Paul is the experience of most people: 'The good which I want to do, I fail to do; but what I do is the wrong which is against my will' (Rom. 7.19).

It is sometimes said that 'ought' implies 'can'; and there is obviously a truth in this. But it is equally true that 'ought' often indicates 'cannot'. I realize my moral responsibility; but somehow or other I am constrained to act irresponsibly. Only a religion that acknowledges a source of grace and power *outside* of man can speak to this condition.

We have allowed the secular and religious moralists to parade their objections to each others' views. As is often the case with prepared speeches, subtleties may have been lost and contrasts drawn too sharply in black and white. That there is some substance to most if not all of the objections can hardly be denied. We could spend a lot more time on trying to adjudicate. However, bearing the objections in mind, let us now go on to see if we can mark out some common ground on which discussion and dialogue would be a profitable enterprise.

DISCUSSION QUESTIONS

Is obedience a virtue?

If, as anthropologists have suggested, religion has functioned as an integrating and validating agency in society, what happens to the morality of a society when a process of secularization occurs?

Is it true that religion fosters moral immaturity?

7

MORALITY AND RELIGION: DIALOGUE

Secular and religious moralists have often seen their respective approaches as antagonistic and irreconcilable. For theists the conflict has sometimes been between a man-centred and autonomous morality on the one hand and a God-centred and heteronomous morality on the other. Thus the conflict is sharpest where religion affirms that the world has been created by God, who has also ordained the laws which his creatures are to obey. In such a tradition the will of God is of primary importance, and obedience to his will is the mainspring of human virtue. God commands; man must obey. Against such a position the secular moralist affirms that man must be free to exercise his own moral responsibility and that the standards of right and wrong, good and bad, are independent and underived. Religious morality reduces responsible human beings to the status of slaves and subordinates the moral standard to the arbitrary, even if self-consistent, decision of Omnipotence.

If there is to be any constructive dialogue, religious moralists must make two things clear: first, that they too respect the proper independence of the moral standard; second, that whatever they feel bound to say about human creatureliness, they have no wish to turn men into either puppets or slaves.

HUMAN NEEDS

Let us take the moral standard first. There are, as we have seen, different ethical accounts of it. Some philosophers have argued that certain actions are right and others wrong, and that men can recognize this fact intuitively. Others have argued, more persuasively, that morality has an object, namely, the amelioration of the human predicament. Rules, principles and virtues are explicable in terms of the purpose which they serve. Different moralities are to be assessed in terms of this purpose. There is no need to go beyond the human facts to decide which morality is preferable to which.

Religious moralists, I suggest, need take no exception to this approach to ethical theory. Indeed, it is an approach which they may well be advised to adopt for themselves. Morality *is* about human beings, their needs and how these needs are to be met. Christians believe that God made the world, yes; but also that in making it he gave it a certain nature. It is this nature which determines the shape and substance of morality. To say that morality is first and foremost about man is not to deny that man is the creation of God—any more than to say that physics is about the natural world is to deny that the natural world is the creation of God. Even God cannot make human nature flourish in a way which is contrary to that human nature. He cannot make and un-make at one and the same time!

In short, there should be no disagreement between secular and religious moralists concerning the logical structure of morality. It concerns human life and human flourishing. Where they will differ is not in their views about the nature of morality, but in their views about the nature of human flourishing and the nature of the world in which the moral enterprise is undertaken.

HUMAN RESPONSIBILITY

What about human creatureliness and human responsibility? Many secular moralists seem anxious to affirm not only that man is morally responsible, but also that he is fundamentally rational, compassionate and good. Many religious moralists, on the other hand, seem equally anxious to affirm that he is morally blind, selfish and sinful, Secular moralists speak of man's freedom of will, religious moralists of man's bondage. Where is there any common ground?

Those who wish to emphasize his freedom are, whatever else they have in mind, determined to affirm that man is responsible for his actions. He is no automaton. If anyone says that he is not responsible for his actions, that he cannot help doing the things he does because that is the sort of person he is, and the person he is is the result of heredity and environment, over which, quite obviously, he has had no control, then the secular moralist will retort that he cannot get rid of his responsibility in this way. Of course, there are some circumstances in which a person cannot be held responsible for what he does. He may be too young, or too distraught, or too ill, to understand what it is that he is doing. Or even if he does understand, there are times when his behaviour is compulsive, so that he cannot control himself even if he tries. But the fact that there are some circumstances in which we do not hold a person responsible for what he does, does not entail that there are no circumstances in which he is responsible. On the contrary, it suggests the very opposite.

The religious moralist, too, is determined to affirm man's responsibility, at least in the sense that he cannot shelve part of the blame for his wrong-doing. He must 'answer' for his sins. What the secularist deplores, however, is any suspicion of a doctrine of man's total corruption. Man is answerable, some preachers may declare, but he is impotent. Everything that God is, man is not. God is strong, man is weak. God is righteous, man is a sinner. God is all, man is nothing. Even man's righteousness is as filthy rags, a vain attempt to cover his sin and to justify his godlessness. So the preacher may attempt to drive his hearer to the limits of self-condemnation and despair, in the hope that at that point he will be ready to throw himself without further question or struggle into the arms of God.

There is no need, however, for the religious moralist to accept the preacher's rhetoric. Certainly man is ignorant and needs to be taught. Certainly he is weak, and his desires are often selfish. When he sees the highest, he does not necessarily desire it, and when he desires it, it is not within his power alone to attain it. He needs guidance and grace. Even so, it by no means follows that he is totally corrupt and utterly impotent. He can still distinguish between good and evil, at least in some instances. He can still, with effort and self-control, set himself to do what he knows to be his duty, at least in some instances. He is neither an imbecile nor a monster.

An interesting parallel can be drawn between the preacher and the cynic. The preacher proclaims that despite all appearances to the contrary man is utterly depraved. Even those actions which, humanly speaking, appear to be good are in fact unpleasing to God, since they stem from a corrupt and sinful heart. The cynic, too, asserts that, however altruistic and unselfish an act may look, it is really done out of self-interest. 'What is the man getting out of it himself?' the cynic asks, and calls in the psychologist to support his view that motives are never what they seem. Cynics flourish because there is a grain of truth underlying their cynicism. Human motives are frequently mixed. Self-interest is more pervasive than many of us care to admit. Often it operates at an unconscious level. Nevertheless, the cynic is wrong. He thrives on our uncertainty. But he is a poor judge of human nature. People do sometimes act unselfishly.[1]

In short, secular and religious moralists may agree on the importance of human responsibility. The measure of man's ability to respond must be assessed in the light of all the facts. There is no need for anyone to distort the facts in the interests of a preconceived theory. If the theist is prepared to grant that God is worshipped, not because he is omnipotent, but because he is good, and that it is part of his goodness to have created man with the ability to make his own judgements and to decide his own actions, then the secular moralist may be prepared to grant that man has still a long way to go before he exercises his freedom responsibly and responsively. Both, then, are agreed that, either with God, if he exists, or without God, if he does not exist, men are called to think and live and act as responsible persons in a responsible society.

BASIS FOR DIALOGUE

Persons matter. This, we suggest, is a basic moral belief which could provide a common starting-point for both secular and religious morality. This is not to say that it is a universal belief.

[1] A classic refutation of the view that all human actions are selfish is to be found in a footnote to Butler's Fifth Sermon, *Upon Compassion*. In it Butler argues against Hobbes' view that 'pity' is a feeling of 'fear for ourselves, proceeding from the sense of another mans calamity'. C. D. Broad has called Butler's argument 'so short and so annihilating ... as [to be] a model of philosophical reasoning'. See C. D. Broad, *Five Types of Ethical Theory* (Kegan Paul, Trench, Trubner and Co. 1934), p. 63f.

In some cultures persons have not been reckoned to matter very much. Kings may have mattered, but not slaves. Nations may have mattered, but not individuals. Whites may have mattered, but not blacks. It is only in certain cultures that it has been taken as self-evident that persons matter. Nevertheless, it is difficult to suggest any other basic moral conviction likely to meet with general acceptance.

Persons matter. They matter to themselves. They matter to others. Perhaps, too, they matter to God. That persons matter could be taken simply as an assertion of psychological fact, usually but not always true. It is intended, however, to be more than that, to be an assertion of 'moral fact', or, if such language is rejected, of intrinsic value. Persons matter, whether they matter to themselves and to others or not. This, at least in part, is what is meant by those who say that persons matter to God. If they matter to him, it follows for anyone who believes that God is good that they *ought* to matter to themselves and to others. Those who do not believe in God may affirm without more ado that persons have an intrinsic value. They might say that persons confront them with an inescapable moral 'claim'.

We have already had occasion to speak of the moral 'claim' when we were discussing the conscience. In the context of morality the language of claim is metaphorical. Claims are normally made on the basis of established legal rights. If I make a claim on my insurance company, the success of my claim will depend on the contract I have entered into with the company and the facts which I adduce in support of my claim. The claim will fail if the contract is invalid or if the facts are not as I say they are.

When we speak of a moral 'claim', there is no comparable contract. The legal framework is missing. Yet the similarity between the moral and the legal situations is such that the language of moral law and moral claim springs naturally to mind. Persons are such that, contract or no contract, we recognize their claim on our regard. The claim arises out of what, as persons, they are.

Respect for persons includes self-respect as well as respect for others. Thus there is an individual as well as a social aspect of morality. Respect for others is widely accepted as a basic moral principle. Self-respect is not so widely accepted, since it is often assumed that an individual has the right to make of his own life whatever he chooses, so long as he does not infringe the similar rights of others. If he wishes to drink himself to death, that is his business. This assumption, however, is open to question.

It is important here to distinguish between morality and law. It may be argued that the law has no right to interfere with an individual's liberty, except in so far as an individual's actions impinge on others, and that if there are no questions of social well-being an individual should be free to do whatever he likes. The law, that is, has a restricted function. But it is another question whether an individual has the moral right to do with himself whatever he likes. The basic moral claim that persons matter may suggest otherwise. If an individual ceased to care about himself, what he did or what happened to him, whether he had any say in his own life or whether he was just the tool of others, we might be inclined to say that he was deaf to the claims of his own humanity. Self-respect must be sharply distinguished from selfishness.

The path from the basic moral claim of respect for persons to an integral morality and a consistent ethical theory is a long one. We have to ask what persons *need* in order to be 'persons', both in themselves and in relation to one another. In order to answer this question, we have to make up our minds what a 'person' is. Is he a sentient animal? Is it then his feelings that matter? Is he a thinking animal? Is it then his purposes that matter? Is he a social animal? Is it then his relationships that matter? Is he all these things and more? Has he the possibility of what is sometimes called self-transcendence, of standing outside of what at any moment he has become and of making his own free decisions how he shall shape what he will become? If so, we must stress his potentiality for freedom and responsibility. We might suggest that a 'person' is a focused centre of feeling and activity, with a point of view of his own in a world which he shares with others.

As we develop some clearer idea of what a person is and what he needs, so we may find ourselves using the concepts of benefit and harm, of flourishing and of being diminished. Apart from their basic and essential needs persons may vary in the ways in which they develop and express their own interests. There is no single pattern of life which is *the* pattern for everyone. Within a common framework of respect for persons and for what contributes to personal flourishing there is room for a variety of expressions of human values.

This is not the place to develop a full-scale ethical theory. Let us return to what we have called the basic moral claim, namely, respect for persons. From this it follows that we ought to do whatever contributes to human flourishing, and to avoid whatever contributes to human diminishment. That is our fundamental moral duty. Congruent with this moral duty are those moral virtues, such as honesty, integrity, openness, humanity, and the like, which find expression in a direct and persistent concern that persons should flourish.

If we can accept this, or something like this, as common ground between the secular and the religious moralist, what contribution can be made to morality by religion? From the way in which we have so far been talking it might seem to follow that morality is not only autonomous, in the sense that it does not need any religious presuppositions in order to get under way, but also self-contained, in that religious considerations have dropped out of sight altogether. Both the form of the moral claim and the content of the moral enterprise seem, at first sight, to be completely independent of any religious belief and commitment.

How religions view the basic moral claim that persons matter will depend in no small part on how they view the goal and process of salvation and how they relate man's secular needs to his religious needs. If the way to salvation is fundamentally a withdrawal from the world, then the links between religious and secular morality will be minimal. Religious conduct will be motivated by a desire to escape from the illusion of the world, and how a man is to behave in the world will be determined by his desire to escape from it. If, however, the world is created and ordered by God, then life in the world is in this regard good, and a concern to meet man's secular needs becomes part and parcel of religious obedience.

In the rest of this chapter, and indeed in the remaining chapters of the book, we shall be singling out, as one important example of the continuing dialogue between morality and religion, the contribution which Christians may consider is made to morality by their specifically Christian beliefs.

Christians share, or should share, the fundamental moral conviction that persons matter. They have no reason to turn up their noses at secular morality simply because it does not refer to the will of God or because it is not specifically Christian. With all its strengths and weaknesses it can be gratefully acclaimed and accepted for what it is, an expression of a shared humanity.

At the same time Christians will want to add something to the secular account. They believe that human well-being, whatever else it may be, is first and foremost a matter of man's relationship to God. Once God is brought into the picture, everything must surely be transfigured, for God is Creator, Redeemer and Fulfiller. Man's moral responsibility receives a new dimension. Everything somehow becomes different.

On this point Christians would, I suppose, in principle and in general agree. But if they tried to spell out more or less precisely what the difference was, agreement would soon disappear. Some might argue that Christian values are almost always a reversal of secular values, that the way of the naturally good man and the way of Christ are opposite ways. Others might argue that secular values are still affirmed by the Christian, but now more vividly and more compellingly. There has always been both a world-denying and a world-affirming strand in the Christian tradition. Yet others have looked for some kind of dialectic or synthesis, in which secular values are in part affirmed and in part transformed, so that there are similarities and differences between Christian and secular ways of life.

Let us begin our comparison by distinguishing between context, motivation and content. We have already admitted that for the Christian morality is set within a different context from that in which it occurs for the secularist. For the Christian 'things' are ultimately on the side of moral goodness, for, whatever the

83

appearances may be, they are under the providential care and control of God. Man is not alone in an indifferent universe which may at any moment bring his moral enterprise down to the ground in dust and ashes. He is in God's world. God reigns; and since God reigns, the Christian may approach the moral enterprise with a basic confidence and hope. So, the Christian may argue, his beliefs about God and the world may be expected to create in him an attitude of heart and mind which dispels some of the anxiety, strain and even despair which can characterize moral endeavour. The moral claim is interpreted as the invitation and command of God; and if God is an accompanying and an enabling God as well as a commanding God, then morality itself may be seen as part of a divine–human enterprise.

This religiously conceived context of morality, Christians may claim, will not only affect one's basic attitude to the moral enterprise, it will also lead to specifically religious motives for doing what is morally right. The Christian will be motivated to do what is right, not only because he wants human beings to flourish, but also because he is convinced that God wants human beings to flourish and he wants what God wants.

To want what God wants is an aspect of the Christian's love of God, his recognition of God's glory and his gratitude for the gifts of God's grace. Thus it is not open to the charge of disguised self-interest, such as can be levelled against the religious motive of a fear of the consequences if one does not do what God commands. Nor is it necessarily open to the charge of loving one's neighbour solely because God wants one to love one's neighbour. There seems to be nothing morally objectionable about loving one's neighbour for his own sake and for God's sake, or, as it is sometimes said, loving one's neighbour in God. Nor does there seem to be anything very objectionable about loving one's neighbour for God's sake on those occasions when it is very difficult to love him for his own sake!

We have seen how it may be argued that a Christian context of belief may affect both attitude and motivation. How about the content of morality?

Here Christians hold different opinions. There are those who argue that secular and Christian moralists have the same resources for judging, on the basis of justice and benevolence, what minimizes human harm and maximizes human benefit. Agreement extends, in principle, from the basic moral platitudes, which are the necessary conditions of any co-operative living, for example, that it is wrong to steal, or that it is right to tell the truth, to the principles, virtues and patterns of life which constitute human flourishing. Others, however, argue that, once one goes beyond the basic platitudes, moral differences occur because of different beliefs concerning the nature and destiny of man and the different patterns of life which are commended on the basis of these beliefs. It is sometimes said, for example, that one's assessment of the morality of suicide will differ radically according to whether one believes that men are God's creatures or not. For the Stoics suicide could be seen as a noble act of self-determination in the face of overwhelming disaster or disgrace; for Christians, on the other hand, suicide has usually been seen as an affront against the God who gave men life and who alone has the right to dispose of their dying. However, not all secularists would necessarily agree with the Stoic view; nor would all Christians necessarily be of one mind concerning the morality of suicide in certain abnormal circumstances.

BEING AND BECOMING

Another argument for a difference in content between Christian and secular morality might take the following form. Secular morality, it might be alleged, takes men very much as they are. Consequently, when it comes to a question of their well-being, each man is reckoned to be the best judge for himself. Who am I, or anyone else, to tell you what your true interests are and in what your well-being consists? Of course, if we live in the same community, we must share some moral opinions in order to make it possible for us to live together in harmony. However, within this context—based on what we have called the moral platitudes—it is up to each individual to fashion his own ideal way of life and to pursue his own interests.

Christian morality, however, the argument would continue, has in mind not only what men already happen to be, but also what God calls them to become. It is not only the fact that they have to live in some sort of harmony with one another that places moral restrictions on the free play of their wishes; it is also the fact that they are called to become members of God's kingdom. Thus their interests must not be assessed in terms of their present wishes and self-understanding, but in the light of God's purposes for them. They have been made in the image of God and are called to become conformed to the likeness of God. Thus a sharp distinction between a basic social morality and a variety of individual ideals is one which the Christian moralist finds it difficult to accept. It fails to do justice, to his way of thinking, to the inescapable relation in which man stands to God, whether man recognizes it or not. This relationship is not one which he can choose or not choose, according to his private ideals.

Finally, in considering the content of Christian morality, what are we to make of the demand for perfection implicit in the belief that men are called to become conformed to the likeness of God?

Often we consider our secular moral duties to be limited. The claim of respect for persons goes so far, but no further. A good man will no doubt do more than his bare duty; but we have no right to demand of him that he do so. Even our hopes that he will do so are contained within the bounds of what it is reasonable for us to expect of him. Morality is more insistent on the duty of avoiding harm than the duty of promoting the good.

Christian morality apparently breaks down the limits which we normally recognize. There are to be no limits to love and forgiveness. If forgiving seven times stretches our notion of what is our duty, forgiving seventy times seven shatters it in pieces. Christians are called to love their neighbours in the way in which God loves man—without limit and without considerations of desert.

This element of perfectionism has been condemned on both moral and psychological grounds. It has been said that some men are not worth loving. It has also been said that to seek perfection is the surest way of becoming a hypocrite: in aiming too high a man achieves less than he would have done if he had aimed lower.

Christians, however, cannot escape this challenge to perfection. The demands of love go well beyond the demands of ordinary

86

duty. They have been taught this lesson time and time again. Where, perhaps, they run into trouble is in any attempt to make love an extra and especially laborious kind of duty. No doubt the love of God and the love of neighbour are what is 'due' to God and neighbour. But they cannot be deliberately engineered. They are not at the disposal of our hearts and minds. Hence the challenge to perfection is first and foremost a call to see life in a new light, thus evoking a new response. Love demands, but only because Love first gives. So duty may be transformed into delight. In the words of a Christian prayer, 'Grant unto thy people, that they may *love* the thing which thou commandest, and *desire* that which thou dost promise; that so, among the sundry and manifold changes of the world, our hearts may surely there be fixed where *true joys* are to be found.'

Whatever we may think of the way in which this argument is developing, we cannot but observe that the Christian moralist is here again appealing to the total context in which he sees human life and the moral enterprise. The context is one in which God's grace precedes man's response. Thus whatever it may be that distinguishes Christian morality from its secular counterpart is to be traced back to the beliefs which the Christian holds concerning God, man and the world. Morality, it is agreed, concerns the well-being of man; but for the Christian the well-being of man is grounded in the good will of God. Hence it is to the idea of the will of God that we next turn our attention.

DISCUSSION QUESTIONS

Is the moral conviction that persons matter strengthened in any way by the religious conviction that they matter to God?

'Be ye perfect, as your Father in heaven is perfect' (Matt. 5.48). What does the idea of Christian 'perfection' involve? Is it an idea that can be defended against the charge of exaggerated romanticism?

Does religion enlarge or restrict our understanding of what it is to flourish as a human being?

8

THE WILL OF GOD

Morality and religion, we have argued, need not be in conflict. In practice, religious conviction and passion have sometimes added fuel to the fire of man's inhumanity to man, but at other times they have been instruments of reconciliation and peace. In principle, too, a case can be made out for the view that religion complements rather than undermines morality.

Those who believe in God ground the moral claim in his will. When they are considering what they ought to do, they may sometimes ask themselves what God wants them to do. Probably they will not always ask this question. On ordinary moral problems they may make their own judgements in ordinary moral terms: there is no need to refer everything directly back to the will of God. In difficult cases, however, or when it comes to a matter of fundamental principle, what God wills becomes the primary question and the ultimate concern.

We have already seen that in appealing to the will of God it is not necessary to admit that morality is in the last resort arbitrary. It may be the case that Thomas Hardy's 'President of the Immortals', when he had finished his sport with Tess, was content to discard her and to turn his attention elsewhere. But the believer's God is not like Hardy's President. His will is not arbitrary, even if it is sometimes said to be inscrutable. Nor need we accept Thomas Hobbes' view that 'the right of God's Sovereignty is derived from his Omnipotence'.[1] Certainly the believer ascribes to God supreme and final authority. But this authority is grounded in God's goodness and grace, not in his power. Nor, again, need the exercise of authority be harsh and 'authoritarian'. As Creator, God will know what man needs and

[1] Thomas Hobbes (1588–1679) is best known for his political masterpiece *Leviathan*.

what is for his well-being. As good and gracious God will desire man's well-being. What is more reasonable, then, for one who believes in God than that, when he is uncertain what he ought to do, he should inquire after the will of God?

If inquiry after the will of God is not necessarily a submission to arbitrary power, neither is it necessarily an admission of infantile dependence. In many situations we consult authorities and act on their opinions. We take it that they know what they are talking about when we do not know. This does not imply that we never use our own minds or make our own judgements. The recognition of another's wisdom, and hence of his authority, is no bar to our own growth and development. If it were, the whole business of education would be rendered 'infantile'! No doubt there are infantile believers who want to be told what God wills in order that they may evade accepting their own moral responsibility; but infantile dependence is not a necessary consequence of believing that God's will is highly relevant to the moral decisions that we make.

More difficult problems arise for the believer when we ask him how he knows what the will of God is.

REVELATION

If he wishes to say more than that, through his reason, man participates in the eternal reason, and that therefore by using his reason he may himself discover what is according to the mind and will of God, he must appeal in some way to revelation. Where human reason is weak, or where there are special divine commands which are in principle unknown to human reason, God himself reveals what is according to his mind and will. Thus revelation overlaps with, and at the same time goes beyond, the area which unaided human reason can explore and map. Basil Mitchell has expressed this overlap and complementarity in the form of a parable which he constructed in order to show that there was nothing basically wrong with a believer's appealing both to secular moral arguments and to revelation when trying to solve some complex moral problem:

We have reason to believe that our King is very wise and

that is why we accept his authority. Our independent investigations in social science lend support to this belief of ours, in so far as we are able to rely upon them, although we do not make the mistake of supposing that our social scientists are omnicompetent. We have need, of course, to interpret the King's commands, so as to apply them intelligently to the changing problems of our society and we find it a useful rule to interpret them in such a way that they make sense. In doing this we receive valuable help from the King himself.[2]

An appeal to revelation itself raises difficult problems, not least the problem of discriminating between different and conflicting 'revelations'. How are we to know which of the claimants is the true one? Believers have developed several answers to this question which we cannot go into here. Problems concerning the grounds for religious belief are some of the most difficult problems that a believer has to face. However, part of any answer is likely to include the claim that our ordinary moral insights, which we possess simply because we are human beings and independently of any religion or revelation, provide some criterion for deciding whether an alleged 'revelation' is in fact a revelation of God. Consequently, it is a mistake to oppose reason and revelation, as if revelation were something completely separate from reason. Reason cannot be bypassed in this way.

GOD'S COMMANDS

Let us suppose that a case has been made out for believing that God has in fact revealed something of his will and purposes to man, and that 'the Maker's instructions' are to be found in certain sacred writings. In these writings there is a Law of God which those who accept the authority of the writings are bound, in allegiance to God, to obey.

If there is a revealed Law of God, it must be made clear what, precisely, that Law is. Christians, for example, have asserted that the writings of the Old Testament contain the revealed

[2] Basil Mitchell, *Law, Morality and Religion in a Secular Society* (O.U.P. 1967), p. 118.

Law of God. Yet in the light of the teaching of Jesus and of the writings of the New Testament they have argued that the ceremonial and ritual parts of that Law are no longer operative. They were valid only for the old dispensation; since the new dispensation they have been rendered invalid.

If ceremonial commands can be valid only for a limited period, cannot the same be said of certain moral commands? Take, for example, the practice of divorce. This seems to have been sanctioned by the law of God as revealed in the Old Testament (cf. Deut. 24.1). Jesus, however, is said to have taught that God's original will was that marriage should be indissoluble, and that divorce had been permitted in certain circumstances only because of the hardness of men's hearts (cf. Mark 10.2f.). Some Christians have argued from this that what God once permitted he no longer permits: his Law has been made more rigorous. Others have argued that Jesus was distinguishing between God's will and the Law: it was a fundamental error to believe that if one had kept the Law one had thereby lived in accordance with God's will. In breaking the marriage bond divorce was no different from adultery: at the best it could be counted only as a necessary evil.

Further difficulties in establishing which are the revealed commands of God are occasioned by the nature of some of God's alleged commands. Can God really have commanded Abraham to sacrifice his only son Isaac (Gen. 22.2)? Can he really have commanded Saul to exterminate the whole tribe of the Amalekites, 'man and woman, infant and suckling, ox and sheep, camel and ass' (1 Sam. 15.3)? Had these commands been issued by any human being, we should have had no hesitation in condemning them as wicked. They would be no less wicked if in fact they had been issued by God. But God is not wicked. Therefore they cannot have been issued by God. Consequently, we cannot take at its face value the claim that God on these occasions revealed his will. If we cannot take the claim at its face value here, can we be sure that we are right to take it at its face value anywhere else? Must we not use our moral discrimination as a test of the authenticity of any claim to express God's revealed Law?

Such moral discrimination is in fact already being exercised within the biblical tradition itself. For example, a deed which in an earlier tradition is attributed to the inspiration of God (2 Sam. 24.1) is in a later tradition attributed to the inspiration of Satan (1 Chron. 21.1). Clearly the later editor could not accept the view that God would himself directly instigate an action which was sinful.

If God's revealed will is to be effective and authoritative, it must be clearly communicated by someone whom we recognize as God's law-giver. If there is doubt concerning the content and extent of God's revelation, then we find ourselves in the following dilemma. We have to decide whether a particular command is in fact God's command. If it accords with our own moral sensitivity, then we may have reason to accept it as authentic. If it does not so accord, then we may have no reason to accept it. Indeed, in some instances the discrepancy between the command and our own moral judgement may be so great that we have good reason not to accept it. But if this is the case, of what value is God's revelation of his will? It was suggested earlier that its value lay in its informing and instructing us when our own moral reason was somehow inadequate to do the task. But in so far as we are prepared to accept as authentic only those commands which concur with our moral reason, such value turns out to be little or nothing.

If there are difficulties about recognizing God's revealed commands, there are also, as Basil Mitchell admits in his parable, difficulties about interpreting them. They may be so general that they do not throw much light on the particular moral problem that confronts us here and now. Or they may be so specific to the time, place, persons and culture in which they were first communicated that their wider and abiding significance is far from obvious. In any case, given a set of divine commandments, there is also a need for casuistry, that is, for the application of the commandments to different situations. Different teachers will produce different interpretations, and so the desire for certainty, which was one of the motives for welcoming the idea of a revealed divine law, will be disappointed.

Once again we see the important part played by reason in interpreting revelation. The commands of God have to be interpreted 'in such a way that they make sense' in the present situation. Even so, it does not follow that the revelation is useless. Reason has something given to it to reflect upon. It is looking in a direction which has been laid down for it. The sense that it makes of this material may differ from the sense that it would have made of experience had not this revelation been available.

Within the Christian tradition this idea of God's revealed Law has sometimes come under severe criticism. It has been said that it has produced a narrow legalism: God himself has disappeared somewhere behind his Law. But God's will presses upon individuals personally in every moral situation. It is concrete and particular, whereas the Law is general and often abstract. Consequently the idea of the will of God must be interpreted in a personal rather than a legal framework. God addresses the individual as directly as one man addresses another. The Law is only one aspect of God's communication with man, and not the most important aspect at that.

Hence it is a mistake to look to the Scriptures in order to discover what God is commanding in any particular situation. They provide signposts, suggestions, indications, but not universal and unexceptionable rules. God's command cannot be reduced to a principle or a rule; it is immediate and direct. As Karl Barth puts it: 'It is always an individual command for the conduct of this man, at this moment and in this situation; a prescription for this case of his ... It leaves nothing to human choice or preference. It thus requires no interpretation to come into force. To the last and smallest detail it is self-interpreted.'[3]

Barth is very different from Butler, who believed that a Christian's moral duty could be discerned by reflecting on the proper nature of man. Nevertheless he shares with Butler something of the same sense of the immediacy of the final moral decision. For Butler it was the intuitive recognition of what an ordered human nature required; for Barth it is the immediate apprehension of what God commands. For neither is there any question of arbitrariness or irrationalism. There is a proper place for reflection, in one case on the principles of self-love and benevolence, in the other case on the witness of the Scriptures. But reflection cannot of itself produce the moral answer; in the

[3] K. Barth, *Church Dogmatics* III/4:11–12. Quoted in Gene Outka, *Agape* (Yale University Press 1972), p. 230.

end there is the judgement of conscience or the decision of obedience.

This element of immediacy in the self-communication of God to man is emphasized in an extreme way by those who believe that they can become aware of God's will without any protracted process of reflection. They may claim to be specially guided by the Holy Spirit, perhaps through prayer. Humanly speaking, it is the non-rational part of man's make-up that provides the medium for God's communication. God's spirit 'touches' the human spirit, dispels perplexity and prompts action.

Can one be sure, however, that this movement deep within the human spirit is the prompting of God? Do we not have to 'discern the spirits'? Are there not forces at work within our unconscious which are very far from being the spirit of God? Even if reflection cannot take us the whole way to moral decision, must it not be allowed to play an important part in our coming to a decision? In prayer, it may be said, we allow our whole selves, and not only our minds, to be instrumental in making our final decision; but it must be our whole selves, including our minds, and not only an isolated part of ourselves.

GOD'S PURPOSES

There is another way, it has been suggested, in which it is possible to come to know what is the will of God. Paul Lehmann, for example, has argued[4] that, if Christians are correct in believing that God is active in history, then sensitivity to what he is doing offers a more appropriate way of discovering and responding to his will than any application of revealed laws or claim to inward and immediate inspiration and guidance. In this approach emphasis is placed on the aims and purposes of God in history. These have been pre-eminently set forth in the Messianic activity of Jesus Christ, and with this norm in mind Christians are to exercise an 'imaginative and behavioral sensitivity to what God is doing in the world to make and to keep human life human, to achieve the maturity of men'.

Lehmann's approach has been taken up by other thinkers who have attempted to establish criteria by which one may distinguish

[4] See, for example, his *Ethics in a Christian Context*. S.C.M. Press 1963.

what God is doing from everything else that is going on. Some, especially in Latin America, where the Church has discovered itself willy-nilly in a revolutionary situation, have combined the notion of God's political activity in the world with a Marxian analysis of the course of events, claiming in this way to add to their theological interpretation of history a scientifically valid account of the forces which move men and nations in certain ways rather than in others.

It is possible to argue that an approach which starts from an attempt to discern the purposes of God in history is likely to be more dynamic and more open than an approach which starts from certain given laws. But similar difficulties arise. How do we know what God is doing in the present situation? If we say that he is doing the things which are making human life more human and more mature, have we said anything specific, or have we still to spell out what counts as 'human' and 'mature'? And in spelling out these concepts do we fall back on our ordinary moral insights, or is something special contributed, say, by the person of Jesus as the exemplar of humanity and maturity? Furthermore, even if we are right in thinking that it is possible to discern the main thrust of the divine activity, we are still faced with the particular problem how we are to respond as individuals in this or that particular situation. There is no escape from moral reflection and judgement.

If we are convinced that we have access to a clearly distinguishable set of divine commandments which constitute a divine Law, and also that we have a divinely authorized method of interpreting and applying the Law, then we may appeal with confidence to the revealed will of God. If, however, we are not so convinced, then our appeal to the will of God will not dispel our doubts or solve our moral problems. What it will do is to set them in a context in which we believe that our moral life is part of our total response to the divine initiative, and we shall use those methods of reflection, judgement and decision which seem to us to do most justice to both our moral and our religious experience. We shall not be able to say for certain in any particular situation that we know what the will of God for us is; but it does not follow from this that the whole notion of inquiring after the will of God is necessarily empty or idle.

95

When Christians think in terms of God's will, they are affirming implicitly that there is a created order, the recognition and approval of which will fulfil human life in a way which nothing else can. To find this order, the order of God's kingly rule, is to find a pearl of great price. It is worth selling everything else, even one's most treasured possessions, in order to acquire it. No doubt there are other goods, but this is the *summum bonum*, the supreme good. It is an order that penetrates to the depths of things and does not only reflect patterns on the surface. Consequently it is not easy to discern. Human beings may need God's help, his revelation, in order to recognize it. When they have recognized it, they may need God's further help if they are to succeed in living in accord with it. Nevertheless, life in accord with it is life indeed. Hence the goodness of God becomes the criterion of all goodness, and to inquire after his will is to set out on the path that leads to eternal life.

In tracing the pattern of this divine order Christians may find themselves speaking the moral language of rules and consequences, of ideals and virtues, and the religious language of obedience and discipleship, covenant, law and grace. There is no single correct language or single correct method. In R. B. Braithwaite's words: 'In the context of Christian ethics, a Christian does not love his neighbour *only* to secure joy, peace, the *visio Dei*; but neither does he do so *only* to obey a Kantian imperative; he does so in order to become a member of the Kingdom of Heaven; that is, he opts for one total universe rather than for another.'[5] Some might want to add at this point that the reason why he opts for this universe is because he believes that it is as true a picture of *the* universe as man can have.

In addition to the content which is given to the idea of the will of God in terms of the goods which define his kingly rule, the idea can also have a regulative function. Negatively, it can prevent the believer from identifying any of his own norms with the absolute good. The will of God stands for that perfection

[5] In Ian T. Ramsey, ed., *Christian Ethics and Contemporary Philosophy* (S.C.M. Press 1966), p. 92.

to which his own insights and judgements can only approximate. Positively, it can give grounds for hope that goodness will in the end prevail. The will of God is not frustrated, although it may be hindered, by the failure and disobedience of his creatures. God can turn even the wrath of man to his praise and can re-create when the created order is broken.

GOD'S LOVE

We have spoken of the will of God in terms of obedience to commands and in terms of co-operation with aims and purposes. The concept opens up yet another possibility, that of some kind of personal relationship between God and man, some kind of union of wills, whereby the influence of God penetrates into the very being and response of his human creatures. We move here to language about the 'prevenient'[6] and 'accompanying' grace of God or the indwelling of God's Holy Spirit.

Problems at once arise concerning man's freedom and responsibility. How can his actions be his and God's at one and the same time? Is there not a risk of man's being reduced to a puppet, moved about by the 'hand' of God? We shall be returning briefly to this question in our last chapter. Here we shall content ourselves with putting forward the suggestion that we may on occasions accept full responsibility for the particular decisions that we make, and yet at the same time affirm that we should not have been able to make that decision had it not been for the close influence, support and even prompting of somebody else. We make a mistake, perhaps, in isolating the moment of 'making' the decision from the process of listening, responding, reflecting, attending, of which the 'making' is a kind of final shaping and crystallization. Thus a lot more goes into the decision than what I myself directly contribute; nevertheless it is my decision and nobody else's.

When we speak of a close personal relationship between God and man, in which the divine grace goes before, with and after human decisions, the most natural language to use is the language of love. For it is in human relationships of love that

[6] The word 'prevenient' is derived from the Latin *praevenire*, 'to come in front of', or 'to precede'.

97

the closest unity of will with will is achieved. We turn now, therefore, to consider the idea of love, especially love in action, as a key concept in religious and, in particular, Christian morality.

DISCUSSION QUESTIONS

'How do you *know* what is the will of God?' 'You don't; and that is the giddy joke.' If this answer is right, why should a believer bother about the will of God?

Can a Christian discover what the will of God is by asking himself 'What would Jesus have done in this situation?'?

Consider the moral implications of the Abraham and Isaac story (Gen. 22).

9

LOVE IN ACTION

'Love, and do what you will' (Augustine of Hippo, 354–430).
These words of Augustine have become something of a catch-
phrase in certain Christian circles. They are used to utter a
protest, not only against the complex theories of moral philosophers and theologians, but also against the whole collection of
'Do's' and 'Don'ts' which seem to encumber, if not actually
define, the Christian life. They represent a desire to let the fresh
air enter into human and Christian relationships, to sweep away
all the dead wood which has come down from bygone ages, to
discover the one thing needful and to reaffirm a basic simplicity
and responsiveness.

The protest and the desire join together in an appeal to the
primacy of love, a primacy which supersedes all other moral
considerations. Is it not clear to believer and unbeliever alike
that it is love which builds up human relationships and com-
munities, recognizes that persons matter, and proposes the single
goal of human flourishing? If only people loved one another,
would not the conflicts of differing interests soon be resolved?
Is not love a central concern of almost all the religions? Is it not
the fulfilment of the moral law? Cannot the whole of the law be
summed up in the single commandment to love? Away, then,
with all the paraphernalia of rights and duties and rules and
obligations. Let us respond to each situation as it comes along,
with love and with love alone.

'Love, and do what you will.' What Augustine meant by these
words is a matter of some controversy.[1] In the sermon in which
they occur he was arguing that, although it had been his Christian

---

[1] See G. R. Dunstan's discussion in Ian T. Ramsey and Ruth Porter, eds,
Personality and Science (Churchill Livingstone 1971), p. 108f.

duty to call in the imperial forces to protect the Church against the schismatic Donatists, it would have been wrong to do so in any spirit of hatred. Everything that a Christian does by way of duty must be done in a spirit of unalterable love. If this is the correct interpretation of his words, then Augustine was speaking about the basic attitude and disposition which Christians must have; he was not suggesting necessarily that love itself is a sufficient criterion of what a Christian ought to do. To put it another way, love dictates directly the 'how', not the 'what'.

Some have argued that love not only dictates the 'how', but also determines the 'what'. Those who are impatient with reason and reflection may speak of love's 'homing instinct'. Love, that is, instinctively knows what is the right thing to do in a particular situation. There is no need for protracted and tortuous argument. In this sense an appeal to love may resemble an appeal to the immediate utterances of conscience. Both have the attractions and dangers of a short-cut.

SITUATION ETHICS

Others have worked out a more elaborate ethic of love, which does not leave decisions to the immediate feelings and instinctive responses. Joseph Fletcher, for example, has suggested six propositions which define a plausible love-ethic.[2] They are: 1. that only one 'thing' is intrinsically good, namely, love, and nothing else at all; 2. that the ruling norm of Christian decision is love, and nothing else; 3. that love and justice are the same, since justice is love distributed; 4. that love wills the neighbour's good, whether we like him or not; 5. that only the end, and nothing else, justifies the means; and 6. that love's decisions are made situationally, not prescriptively. (Fletcher means by this last proposition that moral decisions must be made anew in the light of each particular situation, not in accordance with an already established rule to which the situation is then conformed.)

What are we to make of this widespread appeal to love alone? We shall begin our comments by looking at some of the underlying dissatisfaction which has given rise to it. Then we shall

[2] See his *Situation Ethics*. S.C.M. Press 1966.

ask whether it offers a more adequate understanding of morality than other theories do.

First, persons, it is urged, are more important than principles. Morality should be made for man, not man for morality. If one makes one's moral decisions simply on the basis of established rules and principles, then persons, with their rich individuality, their special needs and interests, are being treated simply as cases. Their uniqueness vanishes. They become instances of a type, members of a class, numbers in a system. So the first cause of dissatisfaction with traditional ethical systems is the feeling that they are forcing individuals into artificial moulds. Rules must be rules for everyone; but 'I' am not 'everyone', I am uniquely myself. Now love is person-centred. It cares for the individual as an individual, in all his uniqueness, not as one of a kind. No two individuals are alike; therefore they ought not to be treated alike.

Secondly, it is said, morality is concerned primarily with duty. Duty, however, is a restricted concept. It goes so far but no further. Furthermore, a man may do his duty whatever his underlying attitude may be. Love, however, prompts a person to go well beyond the bounds of duty. It is perfectly proper to insist that a man should do his duty; but there are actions which exceed duty—they are sometimes called 'works of supererogation'— which we cannot insist on being done, although we esteem them highly and praise a person for doing them. For example, we can demand that a soldier should not show cowardice in the face of the enemy; but we cannot demand that he should show outstanding bravery. The Victoria Cross is not awarded to someone who has simply done his duty, but to someone who has done more than could reasonably have been expected of him. So love addresses itself to others' needs, not to their rights. When husband and wife begin to talk about their rights, love has already flown out of the window!

Again, love has a spontaneity, an unexpectedness, a creativity of its own. It seeks new ways of meeting others' needs. The strict observance of rules, or even the rational calculation of consequences, is all too liable to quench the living flame which is the heart of love.

Thirdly, situations themselves change. Moral rules which may

at one time have had a valid point and purpose become outdated and no longer serve the needs of people. Changed situations demand changed responses. For example, the discovery
of foolproof methods of contraception cannot but put in question
rules of sexual behaviour which assumed that sexual intercourse
was as likely as not to result in conception. Or, again, the pro-
liferation of nuclear weapons with their devastating effects raises
again the question of the morality of war even in self-defence.
If, then, rules can become outdated, so as to call, in changed
circumstances, for action which is no longer obviously the morally
right thing to do, would it not be better to have a single ultimate
rule, or principle, namely, to do the most loving thing possible?

With much of this argument most people will probably agree.
Morality is for persons, not persons for morality. Love does take
us beyond what we ordinarily conceive to be our duty. Life without spontaneity would hardly be a human life at all. Situations
do change, and what is right in one situation is not necessarily
right in another. Love, in short, does seem to sum up and complete the Law.

Questions, however, must be asked. Granted that individuals
are in some sense unique, is it not as important from the moral
point of view that we should recognize the ways in which they
resemble each other as the ways in which they differ from each
other? John may be white and James may be black; but this
difference is irrelevant if it is a question whether either of them
should be treated as a slave. Mary may be pretty and Molly may
be plain; but this difference is irrelevant if I am deciding which
of the two needs my help in doing her shopping. Some differences
between individuals are morally significant, others are not. The
fact that each individual is in a sense unique is precisely what
gives rise to the basic moral equality between individuals. However much they may differ in intelligence, or strength, or beauty,
they have the same fundamental moral rights and must be given
the same fundamental regard. The presumption, therefore, is that
they are to be treated in the same way, unless the differences
between them are such as to justify their being treated differently.
If love is to be other than liking, or preference, it must recognize
the claims of equality.

Consider, next, the matter of spontaneity. In personal relationships spontaneity is obviously of importance. In being spontaneous we are responding without inhibition; that is, we are not holding ourselves back in any way. This, no doubt, is all to the good. Furthermore, in such relationships, especially when we know each other well, we may often 'perceive' what is for the best without having to give the matter careful thought. Our spontaneity stems from a mutual understanding and a deep, if inarticulate, knowledge. However, this is not always the case, even in close personal relationships. Our spontaneous reactions may, on reflection, turn out to have been misguided. We should have stopped to think. Had we done so, we might have acted more wisely. Moreover, when we move beyond close personal relationships, or when we find ourselves in situations which are very different from anything that we have experienced before, then love itself demands that we should stop and think. Love needs to be guided by the truth, and it is through our thinking that we come to discriminate between what is true and what is false.

Consider, lastly, the matter of moral rules. Certainly rules may become outdated and need to be changed. It does not follow from this, however, that it would be better to do without all rules except the single 'rule' of love.

Rules have various functions in human life. For example, they may embody the wisdom of the past. If so, they can be expected to express the wisdom for the present, unless there are good reasons for thinking that change has rendered them invalid.

Or they may be part and parcel of a social convention, such as promising, without which human life would be very much the poorer. Making a promise is an act which commits one to doing what one promised. That is what promises are all about. They add a measure of reliability to human co-operation. In certain circumstances it may, for weighty moral reasons, be morally justifiable to break one's promise; but this must be the exception rather than the rule. The rule must be that everyone who makes a promise is bound to keep his promise. What is more, this rule must be strictly observed. We all favour ourselves, and it is only too easy for me to think, when keeping my promise is going to cause me trouble, that I shall be justified in breaking it, mine being quite clearly one of those exceptional cases which we are all in principle prepared to recognize.

103

Again, a rule may be justified on the grounds that more good will be achieved if everyone keeps the rule than if everyone makes up his own mind what is for the best. In some cases it would in fact be for the best if the rule were broken. But if there were no rule, then there would be more cases in which people, either through ignorance or through moral blindness, acted in a way contrary to what was for the best.

Finally, there is the question, which we raised before when we were considering an ethic of consequences, whether there are some kinds of action which ought to be ruled out altogether. Some would say, for example, that there are some actions, such as torturing women and children, which are so inhuman that absolutely nothing could justify them. Or, a slightly different case, it might be argued that there were some actions which were always wrong *under normal conditions*. It might be conceivable that, in highly exceptional circumstances, it would be right for an advocate deliberately to deceive the jury. Under normal conditions, however, such behaviour would always be morally wrong. And moral rules are intended to operate against a background of normality, not in conditions which confront men with agonizing and impossible choices.

LOVE'S DYNAMIC

Let us now look more closely at the recommendation that love, and love alone, should be taken as the beginning and end of morality.

What is this love? Is it a feeling, or an attitude? Is it something we experience from time to time, or is it a settled direction of our hearts and minds, expressed in action when occasion demands? If the latter, as, I imagine, most of us would affirm, then we must note that acting out of love is not the same thing as acting as at any moment we may feel like acting, however strong our feeling may be.

What sort of attitude is love? I may say that I love chocolate, I love my dog, and I love my wife. I love them all, but I do not love them all in the same way. I love chocolate because it tastes good, and I eat it whenever I get the chance. I love my dog because my dog loves me and invariably greets me when

I come home. I look after him, see that he is properly fed and take him for walks. In short, I consider his needs as long as I need him. What about my wife? Do I love her because I need her? Or do I love her simply because she is the person she is and I want to give her the moon?

There is a needing love and a giving love. They are sometimes designated by two Greek words, *eros* and *agapē*. *Eros* is a love which desires because it needs. So it seeks to fill up a gap, to get what it wants. *Agapē* is a love which overflows. It gives rather than grasps, and seeks nothing for itself, everything for the beloved. *Agapē* is the word which is used in the New Testament especially of God's love for man. It is also used in the summary of the Law for man's responsive love of God and for his love of his neighbour.

Agapē, presumably, is the love which is advocated as the source and spring of morality. It has been described in a number of ways. It is a regard for another person which is independent of that person's qualities, attainments or merits. It is therefore constant and unalterable. It is a turning from oneself to another for the sake of the other. It is self-forgetful and self-sacrificial.

What is the relation of such love to justice? Certainly it could never countenance injustice. Does it go beyond justice? Our answer will depend in part on our understanding of justice. If we take justice to mean the principle that everyone should be treated according to his deserts, then there is a gulf between love and justice, for love is not disposed to determine action in the light of deserts. If, however, we take justice to mean the principle that everyone should be treated according to his needs, then love and justice are closely connected. Ordinarily, however, we are inclined to contrast love with justice; justice operates within defined limits, whereas love does not. Even so, it is arguable that love cannot be content with anything less than justice, and that in many spheres justice is the most that love can be expected to achieve.

LOVE'S OBJECTIVE

Love as a basic set and direction of the heart and mind, as the attitude which Augustine called for when he said 'Love, and do

105

what you will', demands wisdom and understanding if action is to be an adequate expression of attitude. If love is directed towards the neighbour's needs, then the most loving action will not only be concerned about the agent's motive, but will also embrace his intention and purpose, for it will be concerned with discovering what it is that meets the neighbour's needs and ministers to his well-being. Where there is more than one neighbour, love will be concerned with the needs and well-being of them all. Since love can be misguided, a loving attitude does not necessarily lead to a loving act. A mother, motivated by love, may inadvertently swamp her child with her attention and prevent him from growing into an independent and responsible adult.

Since loving action must be determined primarily in terms of others' needs, to answer the question 'What ought I to do?' with the advice 'Do what love bids you do' is to give no answer at all. In the same way the answer 'Obey your conscience' would be no answer, unless it serves to remind a person that he should make up his own mind and not have it made up for him by somebody else. This, however, may not be the point that he is worried about. Rather he is asking for advice about *how* to make up his own mind.

When love asks the question what action is to be taken in the name of love, all the ethical problems which we have been considering have still to be faced. Is the love-ethic to be identified with an ethic of consequences, even with a utilitarian ethic, as Mill asserted: 'In the golden rule of Jesus of Nazareth, we read the complete spirit of the ethics of utility. To do as you would be done by, and to love your neighbour as yourself, constitute the ideal perfection of utilitarian morality.'[3] Does the well-being of persons in a community demand that other considerations be taken into account than the production of the greatest amount of happiness? Is there a variety of human goods? If so, what are we to do when they conflict with one another? If love is the greatest good of them all, how does one foster in others the ability to love? The problems which these and similar questions raise are not solved by an appeal to love and love alone, for this very appeal itself raises them in another context. What kinds of action,

[3] John Stuart Mill, *Utilitarianism*. In the Everyman's Library edition (Dent 1910), p. 16.

rules and principles, what kinds of virtues, habits and dispositions, make for the flourishing of persons in a community of persons? It may be assumed that the appeal to love bypasses all such questions, but the assumption is false. Discussion and argument continue.

If morality is based, as Warnock suggested, on non-indifference to the well-being of human beings as such and is an attempt to extend transient feelings of good-will into abiding principles and practices, then a love-ethic is not something totally distinct from ordinary secular morality. Love includes non-indifference, but at the same time it transcends it. Its demands are more far-reaching and more stringent. At times they can seem unreasonable, for reasonableness is usually construed in terms of fairness: I will take your interests into account if you will take mine into account; but if you neglect mine, then you cannot expect me to consider yours. Thus fairness, and even justice, despite their impartiality, have one of their roots in enlightened self-interest. Love, on the other hand, is rooted in other-interest; if self is to be considered at all, it must be on the basis that my own well-being is a concern of others, not least of God. So love calls into question the moral standards which men more often than not count as reasonable. In this sense love is 'unreasonable'. It goes 'against human nature'.

THE SPRINGS OF LOVE

From the point of view of common sense it might be said that love, unselfish love, is one force in human nature. Complete and consistent selfishness is something which we do not expect to find in any human being. There is usually some chink in his armour. On the other hand love is only one force. There are other incompatible and competing forces. They all seek expression and so have to be held together in some sort of compromise.

The common-sense point of view, however, is not the only possible point of view. One feature of many religions is that they question the common-sense view of reality. They affirm that things are not what at first they seem to be. There is a deeper, underlying order which can be perceived by those whose eyes have been opened and whose minds have been illumined.

It is this underlying order which provides the criterion of what is to count as reasonable in human norms of behaviour. So, for example, the Christian command to love is rooted in the conviction that God is love and that he has made man in his own image. Man's essential nature, then, is in accordance with love. In acting out of love men are being true to what they really are. Love is not only a force in human nature; it is the essential force, it is the source and spring of personal well-being. Those who love—and remember that we are talking about *agapē*—are acting as 'real' persons; in responding to the nature with which and for which they have been created they have already discovered what it is to 'come alive'.

That love is important in human life is something that most people can recognize for themselves. In psychological language it is sometimes argued that love is at the core of human identity. The ability to love is what makes a human being into a person. Furthermore, the ability to love is itself said to be dependent, at least in part, on the fact of having received love. 'I am, because I think', said the philosopher Descartes (1596–1650). But would it not be more accurate to affirm: 'I am, because I am loved'? I become a real person because someone regards me as a real person.

The fact, however, if it is a fact, that love belongs to the very nature of ultimate reality, is not so easily recognizable. Things do not seem to bear it out. But Christians assert that it is so, and they will usually base their assertion on an appeal to revelation. It has been shown to be so in the teaching, life and death of Jesus Christ and in the events and experiences which followed upon his death. This is the Christian claim. Whether the claim is true or not, the nature of the claim must be understood for what it is. It is the claim that in and through this 'revelation' they have come to 'see' things differently and to 'understand' things differently. The pieces have fallen into a different pattern; and although not everything is yet clear, and there are some pieces of the puzzle which do not very easily fit, nevertheless things make more sense when seen and understood in this way than when seen and understood in any other way. The claim, therefore, is that the revelation is not arbitrary or irrational. On the contrary, it makes deep sense. The 'reasonableness' of God may confound human expectations and challenge established canons of reasonableness, but what is glimpsed now will in the end be seen to make full and final sense. The world, including the world of human beings, will be grasped as it really is only when it is grasped in the light of God's creative, redemptive and fulfilling purposes.

If, then, love is of the very essence of created humanity, then the command to love is not for Christians alone, but for all men. It is not a particular and optional norm; it is a universal and essential norm. It applies to all men everywhere and at all times. It is not 'against human nature'. It accords with human nature, as God intends it to be. Man is made by Love and for love.

DISCUSSION QUESTIONS

Consider carefully the relation between love and justice. Is the commandment to love relevant in any way to the ordering of social and political life?

'Love without knowledge is sentimentality; knowledge without love is inhumanity.' Does experience confirm or refute this assertion?

'We do not regard Christianity as a religion which merely preaches the simple moral injunction that men ought to love one another. Rather it is a religion which illumines the tragic fact that, though love is the law of life, no man completely lives by that law' (Reinhold Niebuhr). Do you agree? If so, what is the point of the Christian commandment to love as expressed and developed in the teaching of Jesus?

10

FREEDOM, OBEDIENCE AND RESPONSIBILITY

Freedom and obedience are often set over against each other. The person who is free makes his own judgements and decisions and accepts responsibility for them. The person who is under authority is not free to act according to his own lights but has to do what he is told to do.

There is, however, a type of human relationship in which freedom and obedience cannot be so sharply distinguished from each other. This is the relationship of friendship or love. In such a relationship freedom is actually enhanced by the way in which each is responsive to the other. Neither dominates the other. Nor is there simply a compromise and adjustment of interests. But each is willing to lose himself in his isolated individuality so that he may discover a new self within the shared relationship. There is a responsiveness to what each may become in and through this freedom of self-giving. To describe this responsiveness we may even reintroduce the language of obedience. But now the obedience is no unquestioning submission of one to the other. It is a shared and mutual obedience, a careful listening, a sensitive response to the invitation and challenge of what they may both become through their relationship. Freedom and obedience achieve a measure of integration within a pattern of responsibility and responsiveness.

It is, perhaps, possible to develop such reflections as these so as to provide a religious, or at least a Christian, ethic of response. In this last brief chapter we shall suggest how such a project might look to one who stands within the Christian tradition and has therefore a Christian point of view. The same kind of project can be undertaken for other religious traditions.

The initial objection is likely to be that you cannot extend to the relationship between man and God the ideas of responsibility and responsiveness which apply to relationships between man and man. God, after all, is God; he is not simply another being like a man. Consequently man is absolutely dependent on him, and this means that man owes him an absolute obedience. In reply, however, it may be suggested that men are indeed absolutely dependent on God, since he is their Creator. Nevertheless, it is this same God who seeks to elicit from them, not an unquestioning obedience, but a willing and whole-hearted love. He wants them as sons, not as slaves. Hence it is his grace and not man's arrogance which suggests an ethic of response rather than an ethic of mere obedience.

Thus at the centre of Christian morality is an affirmation of the initiating, accompanying and fulfilling love of God. Christian moral responsibility consists in responsiveness to this divine approach. 'Responsibility affirms: "God is acting in all actions upon you. So respond to all actions upon you as to respond to his action." '[1]

Without this affirmation the command to love becomes a piece of nonsense. With this affirmation it may become a divine–human possibility, an invitation and challenge, a promise of forgiveness and renewal.

MODELS OF DIVINE ACTIVITY

Various images, or models, suggest themselves as we try to give further shape to the idea of the divine Love. We may, for example, think of God as a lawgiver. Or as a planner. Or as a creative artist.

Each of these models—and no doubt there are others too—has something to contribute to the Christian understanding of God's will. God *is* concerned with the ordering of the world, so that it will not collapse in anarchy. He also has his purposes for man and his other creatures: he wills to establish his kingdom. Since he has given the world and man a certain independence and freedom of their own, the working out of his purposes is no longer inexorable; he awaits and evokes the response and co-operation of his creatures; he is as alert to their

[1] H. Richard Niebuhr, *The Responsible Self* (Harper and Row 1963), p. 126.

111

response as an artist is to the potentiality of the medium in which he is working.

These models, however, need to be set alongside one another as complementary. If that of lawgiver is allowed to occupy the centre of attention, then the Christian moral response becomes primarily a matter of obeying God's laws. Frequently these laws are taken as negative. Don't do this, and don't do that. Consequently the prevailing concern becomes that of keeping on the right side of the law. So long as you do that, what else you do is more or less your own business.

So, too, the model of planner tends to subordinate the present to the future, either in this world or in the next. Ideals of this kind, important as they are, can have a narrowing and even distorting effect. The rich variety of present needs and opportunities is forgotten in the enthusiasm of having discovered the single blueprint of the Kingdom.

The model of creative artist, more adequate than the others though it may well be, may nevertheless tempt us to forget the importance of order and continuity in life and the contribution which the dull and the routine may make to personal and communal well-being. Artists are notoriously difficult persons to live with!

These, and other models can be found in Christian tradition. They can also be found in the Scriptures. It is the task of the theologian to suggest a use of models which may yield insight into, and a way through, the problems of morality in each day and age. If he does his work well he may enable others to discern more clearly what God is calling them to do and to be.

The adventure, however, is much too important to leave to the theologian. Everyone is called to participate in it. In this area of responsiveness and responsibility there are no experts whose word is to be accepted without question. No doubt there are those who see more clearly and hear more acutely, but the theist recognizes that the symphony of God's activity is far too rich for any individual or group of individuals, even of any single religious tradition, to appreciate it to the full.

Such, we may suggest, is the shape and form of Christian moral responsibility. We have not suggested in detail what Christians ought to do when confronted with this or that personal or social problem. At the level of particular problems Christians do not always speak with a united voice. Probably such a disagreement is inevitable, and we ought not to be too surprised by it. If the answers to moral problems were always clear, there would not be any moral problems. Nevertheless, Christians are not without their own sources of guidance. They possess a wisdom which they have inherited from the tradition of the past. They also claim to be alert to the prompting of the Spirit of God in the present. By taking counsel together they seek a way of transforming vision and insight into principle and practice. In the end, however, they put their confidence and trust neither in the permanent validity of rules nor in the infallibility of their own insights. They put their confidence in the living and loving God, in whose life they are invited to share and to whose activity they are challenged to respond.

DISCUSSION QUESTIONS

Can persons be committed to each other and at the same time be free?

To what extent should Christians expect their moral convictions to be shared by non-Christians?

What do Christians mean by the 'guidance of the Holy Spirit'? How do they distinguish the *Holy Spirit* from any other spirit?

FURTHER READING

Bartley, W. W., *Morality and Religion.* Macmillan 1971.

Butler, Joseph, *Fifteen Sermons* and *Dissertation on the Nature of Virtue.*

Dunstan, G. R., ed., *Duty and Discernment.* S.C.M. Press 1975.

Fletcher, J., *Situation Ethics.* S.C.M. Press 1966.

Gustafson, J. M., *Can Ethics be Christian?* University of Chicago Press 1975.

Kant, I., *Groundwork of the Metaphysic of Morals* (A valuable translation and analysis is to be found in H. J. Paton, *The Moral Law,* Hutchinson 1948.)

McCabe, H., *Law, Love and Language.* Sheed and Ward 1968.

MacIntyre, Alasdair, *A Short History of Ethics.* Routledge and Kegan Paul 1967.

MacKinnon, D. M., *A Study in Ethical Theory.* A. and C. Black 1957.

Mill, J. S., *Utilitarianism.*

Mitchell, Basil, *Law, Morality and Religion.* Oxford University Press 1967.

Murdoch, Iris, *The Sovereignty of Good.* Routledge and Kegan Paul 1970.

Oppenheimer, Helen, *The Character of Christian Morality.* Faith Press 1965.

Outka, Gene, *Agapē.* Yale University Press 1972.

Outka, G. and Reeder, J. P., eds, *Religion and Morality.* Anchor Books 1973.

Plato, *The Republic,* Book 1 and *The Euthyphro.*

Ramsey, Ian T., ed., *Christian Ethics and Contemporary Philosophy.* S.C.M. Press 1966.

Tillich, Paul, *Morality and Beyond.* Fontana 1969.

Wallace, G. and Walker, A. D. M., eds, *The Definition of Morality*. Methuen 1970.

Warnock, G. J., *The Object of Morality*. Methuen 1971.

Williams, Bernard, *Morality*. Penguin 1973.

Wilson, John, *Ideals*. Lutterworth Educational 1972.

INDEX